THE
KINGDOM ERA
IS HERE!

WHAT OTHERS ARE SAYING ABOUT
THE KINGDOM DRIVEN LIFE

Pastor Sunday Adelaja is one of the most charismatic and down-to-earth people I have ever seen in my life. His principles and values of life are extraordinary. His heart towards God and people is second to nothing - full of love and humility! When I met him for the first time, I was amazed at his person; he was like the "Jesus" you can see. His practical approach to Christianity makes it so real and tangible. No wonder he pastors the largest church in Europe with a congregation of 99% white Europeans. It is such a great privilege to get to know this legend of our time in person.

This book, *The Kingdom Driven Life,* is one of the most practical books I have ever read. After the Bible, I have not come across any other book that is so life-transforming. It is practical, with real life principles that work. This book is a Kingdom manual for Christians who are ready to take the nations for Christ. I mean taking the Gospel of the Kingdom to the ends of the earth.

I can attest that everything written in this book is what Pastor Sunday practices himself, with testimonies abounding everywhere in the country of Ukraine and in over 50 other countries. He has succeeded in destroying religion and establishing great relationship principles with God, and imposing the Kingdom values in the society. You can't afford not to read this book.

Thank you so much, Pastor Sunday Adelaja, for being a light in our generation!

Dr. Bien Sufficient
Medical Doctor, Writer, Motivational Speaker.
Founder/President, Kingdom Lifestyle Movement (KLM).

Wow! Rarely in our time do we get such a masterpiece! A work put together, not out of cultural perspectives, but out of Kingdom principles and downloaded to a man's spirit. *The Kingdom Driven Life* is greatly influencing our generation in an unusual manner. It is filled with amazing testimonies from individuals and organizations that had been influenced by the principles highlighted in it, and who in turn went ahead to influence so many others.

Cultures, environments, nations and societies are being reconditioned and repositioned as a result of the principles outlined here by Pastor Adelaja. I'm personally calling this book a "Revival Manual." Indeed, there's no way you can read it without becoming a mighty instrument of revival in the world around you.

Mwila Mwila
Founder, Ground Takers Foundation (GTF)
South Africa

The Kingdom Driven Life is the most comprehensive book on the Kingdom of God that I have ever read. Through inspiration and depth, it captures one's attention and penetrates the core of one's emotions. By instruction, it satisfies one's need for knowledge and understanding. Finally, through impartation, it unlocks in the heart of the reader a hunger and desire to see "Thy Kingdom come on earth as it is in Heaven". It is has caused me to personally evaluate my life and make adjustments so that I can grow in the knowledge of the Kingdom of God. This book will create a deep awakening within the spirit of anyone reading it. It is like a trumpet blast to all children of God. It is a clarion call to people of God to take their place in every sphere of life in order to redeem the earth.

Philip Isaacs
Director of Isaacs Guidance & Consulting,
Canada

The Kingdom Driven Life is nothing short of extraordinary! In fact it is a challenge to write an endorsement for a "read" that goes far beyond a typical book. I believe that this book is the most insightful book on the Kingdom of God written in our generation – and maybe ever to be written!

When God wants to emphasize something to grow and mature His Body, He rouses someone with that message to speak to the world. Often through a book that becomes a "classic" in their generation. I personally feel that God has used Pastor Sunday Adelaja not only to transform his nation, but to re-introduce the gospel of the Kingdom of God to the world in these last days. It would be a pity for anyone to merely live or be involved in ministerial work, without ever reading *The Kingdom Driven Life*.

Pastor Derek Schneider
President and Founder,
History Makers Academy/History Makers Society

The Kingdom Driven Life is an End-Time book because Pastor Sunday Adelaja wrote extensively on how the seven spheres of our world are to be ministries of the Kingdom of God. It is certain that any nation that applies the principles in this book will definitely experience a total transformation in all spheres. It will call forth the reign of heaven on earth.

If we all in this generation can put into practice the practical principles that are explored and explained in this book, we will in no time reclaim the earth back for God.

Pastor Sunday Adelaja, You are a blessing to this generation and generations to come.

Gideon Idowu
Medical student.

About 130 million books have been published in modern history. However, very few of those have charted a new course for humanity by providing in-depth revelation of the divine purpose for the existence of mankind. This book, *The Kingdom Driven Life*, does that in an amazing way.

In this book, you will find answers to the questions that even the best of theologians, scientists, psychologists and other scholars have not been able to answer. The wisdom and truth it presents comes across in a remarkable way.

Pastor Sunday Adelaja is a man on a mission to change the world and, with this masterpiece, it is only a matter of time before he accomplishes that goal.

Joshua Amatare
Aerospace Engineer, Pastor.

The Kingdom Driven Life couldn't have come at any better time than this, a time I have decided to be the light of the world. To the world, this is an answer. It is a wakeup call to Christians all over the world. Religion will not transform the world. On the contrary, it will continue to limit the power and influence of those who practice it. This book will erase the religion-mentality and cause a mighty change, not only in the Christendom but the whole world. Those who allow this book to transform them will do wonders.

Elizabeth Ekakoro
Engineering student,
Kenya.

The Kingdom Driven Life is a manual. Not just any manual but a manual for a new product, one that has never been produced before -THE KINGDOM. If you want to operate according to Kingdom principles, you must have this manual, *The Kingdom Driven Life*.

One thing I must warn you about is that Pastor Sunday Adelaja has committed a sin here, a sin that God himself is pleased with - he has murdered theology. He has crushed those religious dogmas you have held so dear to your heart for long. So, get ready to be shaken.

If you want to live the Kingdom-driven life, the life that God desires for us, then grab your copy of this book. It has everything you desire to know and much more.

Adebayo Esther Anuoluwapo
Medical student,
Nigeria

THE
KINGDOM
DRIVEN
LIFE

THE
CORNERSTONE
PUBLISHING

SUNDAY ADELAJA

THE KINGDOM DRIVEN LIFE
Thy Kingdom come, Thy will be done on earth…
By Sunday Adelaja

Published by
Cornerstone Publishing
New York
Phone: +1(516)-547-4999
info@thecornerstonepublishers.com
www.thecornerstonepublishers.com
In partnership With
GOLDEN PEN PUBLISHING LTD, UK

Unless otherwise noted, Bible quotations are taken from the Holy Bible, New King James Version. Copyright 1982 by Thomas Nelson, Inc., publishers. Used by permission.

Scripture quotations marked KJV are from the King James Version of the Bible.

Scripture quotations marked NIV are from the Holy Bible, New International version. Copyright © 1973, 1978, 1984, International Bible Society. Used by permission.

Scripture quotations marked AMP are from the Holy Bible, Amplified Version. Copyright © 1954, 1958, 1962, 1964, 1965, Zondervan Publishing House. Used by permission.

Cover design by: Cornerstone Concept and Design
Copyright © 2015 by **Sunday Adelaja**
ALL RIGHTS RESERVED
International Standard Book Number: 978-1-908040-52-7

Printed in the United States of America

Dedication

To the next generation of believers who are tired of the status quo. Those who no more want to do church as usual. Those who thirst and hunger for something more from Christianity. I pray that God will satisfy your hunger through this humble effort.

Acknowledgments

I will like to acknowledge the amazing team who worked together to make this book happen:

To **Abraham and Queen Great** for proof reading, encouragement, and administrative and logistics support.

To **Johnny and Juanita Berguson** for the editing and logistics support.

To **Francis Van Lare** for their effort toward putting marketing strategies together.

To **Bhekisisa Shabangu** who developed press releases and internet marketing plans.

To **Pastor Gbenga Showunmi** and his team at Cornerstone Publishing for consultation and publishing.

Contents

- Focused on the Kingdom
- Teamwork for Success!
- Great Expectations
- Kingdom Prayer

Foreword

S eldom in a person's life are they an eyewitness to a turning point in history.

You have in front of you a very special book. I believe this is one of the top 3 books written in the last 1000 years. In my opinion, it is definitely the best book on the Kingdom of God.

Let me tell you a bit about how I felt when I met Pastor Sunday. He is an unusual man; I find him to be an exceptional Man of God.

World leaders and church leaders have honored Pastor Sunday. Even U.S. President Bill Clinton, in a private moment, told Pastor Sunday that he appreciated the work he was doing. Most importantly, Pastor Sunday has been called and directed by God to extend His Kingdom. Lasting fruit is the evidence of this.

Pastor Sunday believes God has made everyone for a particular and unique purpose. We understand that purpose when we understand the passions that motivate us. By following those passions we can fulfill our Kingdom destiny and take the good news of the Kingdom into the sphere of influence where our passion is leading us. Our passions are God given and help us understand the purposes that God made us to fulfill.

God wants you to fulfill the particular purpose for which he created you. He has put passions in your heart to help you connect in the areas that he has designed you to impact. This book tells you how to discover your destiny and take Kingdom principles to spheres that perhaps only you can address. God has a unique calling for you. That calling is your destiny. The Kingdom Driven Life tells you how to fulfill your destiny

My wife and I were on the platform with Pastor Sunday in Kiev, Ukraine. We were there for a great celebration. Why were we there on the platform for this great celebration? This is a fact of life: Every great man has enemies. Pastor Sunday has enemies. The reason I was on the platform was because I wanted to affirm the fruit from Pastor Sunday's ministry that I was seeing right in front of my eyes. Jesus said, "By their fruits, you will know them." And let me tell you about the fruit! At that very celebration we saw wave after wave of people come to the stage and share what God had done through their lives. They are bringing in a great harvest, the likes of which I have never heard of or seen. These people were testimony of the fruit that Pastor Sunday's ministry has born. The fruit of this ministry is exceptionally good fruit. All spheres of society are being impacted: millions are coming to know Christ, the face of politics is being renewed in righteousness, businesses are being started by believers and are flourishing, and social ills are being addressed. Just one example is that 10,000 people have been set free from addiction to drugs and alcohol. This isn't just a small harvest, it is an abundant harvest. When this type of harvest comes in, we call it revival. That is what I saw in Ukraine. I saw revival– the harvest coming in like I have never seen it come in before.

The gospel of salvation is extremely powerful. This is where the road divides when I compare what is happening in Ukraine to many of the accounts that I've heard about in other sections of the world. What is different? Let's take a look at the United States. We experienced revival; it left us with a church on every street corner. But, culture is not being impacted. Too many of the efforts I've heard about leave the churches full and culture unchanged. When the good news went forward in the first century, it turned the world upside down.

This is what happened to Pastor Sunday in Ukraine. He built

Europe's first and largest mega-church. He had 15,000 people in his mega church, but what was the outcome? Pastor Sunday looked at culture and realized that even though his church was growing large and healthy, the general society was not being impacted. This started Pastor Sunday on a new journey. That journey was to understand the principles of the kingdom and how they related to culture.

That is the key difference between this work and many other works that I have seen. This work is built on living out the good news of the Kingdom, not just proclaiming the good news of salvation. Of course we need the good news of salvation! But we are saved from one place to another place; we are saved from the kingdom of darkness to the Kingdom of Light. We ought to realize that Jesus talked more about the Kingdom than any other thing. Somehow, we have drifted from our purpose that Jesus left for us. That purpose is to impact all spheres around us with the good news of the Kingdom. This is the purpose that we are saved to!

What has happened in United States is that we have churches on every street corner, but we have lost the understanding of how to impact culture. In the New Testament, when the good news went forth, they turned the world upside down. That is what is happening in Ukraine. I believe that God has raised up Pastor Sunday to change history. It's not every day that you meet someone who history will record as being at the forefront of a change as significant as the Reformation. Yet, should the Lord tarry, I believe this is how history will be written. If Jesus does not come back in our generation I think you will see a book entitled "Pastor Sunday, the Man the Myth the Legend". And I'm sure that this book will document a change in eras. That change will be from our current era where people focus on building their church. We could call this the Church Era. The new era will be when churches focus on extending the Kingdom of God. I believe this new era will be called the Kingdom Era. I believe we are entering the Kingdom Era.

Pastor Sunday and the people he has equipped to live the Kingdom Driven Life have succeeded against all odds. God called this black Nigerian to build the largest church in Europe. Ukraine is not as culturally diverse as America is. They do not readily follow people who are black. Simply because of his race, Pastor Sunday encountered an immense amount of opposition. Yet, God always makes a way for us to fulfill those things he calls us to accomplish. God has caused Pastor Sunday to flourish.

What God is doing through Pastor Sunday is changing the face of Ukraine and is beginning to spread around the world. In front of you are the principles that allow this incredible impact for the Kingdom to happen. Millions of people are coming into the Kingdom and millions of people then find their destiny impacting society with the principles of the Kingdom. These principles will impact culture in our neighborhoods, in our workplaces, in politics, and in every dimension of society.

I see the harvest. I have said, "Here I am, God, please send me! Help me to fulfill my destiny of bringing people into the Kingdom and seeing those people use Kingdom principles to change society causing more people to come into the Kingdom of God. Use me to be a history maker! Use me to change history!"

This is why I am lending my voice to this book. It is an important tool to help us fulfill our destiny. I can see you in my mind's eye saying, "Here I am, God, please send me!"

Come! Together let's change how history will be written for the glory of God! Thy kingdom come thy will be done on earth as it is in heaven. Amen.

Johnny Berguson. Founder/President of kingdom.com
Philadelphia USA.
August 2015.

Introduction

"Therefore, since we are receiving a Kingdom which cannot be shaken, let us have grace, by which we may serve God acceptably with reverence and godly fear."
—HEBREWS 12:28

D uring His earthly ministry, Jesus preached only the gospel of the Kingdom. He came to the earth to restore the Kingdom of God to the world. In contrast, the church has been preaching the gospel of "salvation" for decades, teaching believers to take refuge in the church, avoid the world and eventually escape from it. This faulty gospel has reduced the church to a personal remedy and unhealthy "escape" mechanism rather than the total answer to mankind's total need that it is meant to be.

Not only did Jesus Himself preach the Kingdom of God, but He declared: "…this gospel of the kingdom will be preached in all the world as a witness to all the nations, and then the end will come" (Matt. 24:13). It is possible that the Rapture, which Christians are waiting for, will not happen until the church gets it right, until it leaves the "escapist" gospel and preaches the gospel of the Kingdom to every nation. Only this gospel is powerful enough to restore the reign of the King, regardless of culture, false religions, and other seemingly impossible barriers to the truth.

By definition, the word kingdom refers to "the domain where a king rules." It is not enough for Christ to rule in your heart or the hearts of fellow church members. That is not the ultimate domain of the King of Kings. Christ is not the Light of the church; He is the Light of the world (Jn. 8:12). His lordship must be reflected, not just in developing His character within you, but also in your taking His Light to the lost souls in the world: on your job, into your community, your nation, and the nations of the earth.

The scriptures declare that the Kingdom of God is "righteousness, peace, and joy in the Holy Ghost" (Rom. 14:17). These characteristics of the Kingdom are not meant to be demonstrated only by believers in the environment of a cloistered church congregation. (Unfortunately they are not always evident even in church). They are not to be relegated to promoting church programs and activities while ignoring the ills of society. And the primary mandate for every believer is not to work at a job and come to church to pay tithes. It is to find your personal promised land and use it as a platform to impact society with the Kingdom principles Jesus taught.

Jesus means for believers to become salt and light on the earth, extending His Kingdom principles, values, and lifestyle in every sphere of life, wherever we see unrighteousness and darkness prevailing. Righteousness, peace and joy will characterize the entire society where Christians are promoting the priority, principles, and lifestyle of the Kingdom of God. The increase of harvest for the eternal Kingdom is an important outcome of this.

WELSH YOUTH EMPOWERED TO TRANSFORM THEIR NATION

For example, during the famous Welsh revival of 1904, over 100,000 new converts came to Christ, according to estimates of the time. That great move of the Spirit had very small beginnings and yet it became a movement that quickly spread to the four corners of the world. One of the best known leaders of the revival was Evan Roberts, a Christian youth who was an avid student of the Word and theological works of the day. He prayed regularly that God would visit his nation in revival power. Evan Roberts had a deep spiritual experience during prayer, which he shared with the young people of his church, encouraging them to be open to God. This is considered a main catalyst of the revival that followed.

Evan, his brother Dan, and his best friend Sidney traveled around the country sharing the power of God that was igniting their souls. Their meetings broke the conventional and by-passed the traditional—often ministers just sat down unable to preach or even to understand what storm had arrived in their usually sedate temples.

People were changed in so many ways. The crime rate dropped, drunkards were reformed, and pubs reported losses in trade. Bad language disappeared and never returned to the lips of many. It was reported that the pit ponies failed to understand their born-again colliers who seemed to speak the new language of Zion, without cursing and blasphemy. Even the national sports of football and rugby became uninteresting to fans in the light of new joy and direction received by the converts.

Visitors from France, Turkey, the U.S., to name but a few came to visit and caught the flame, passing it on to their countries. Welsh communities throughout the world felt the effects of the powerful move of God sparked by a few young people interceding for their nation, abandoning themselves to God, and sharing their good news. Their primary mandate was not to work at a job and attend church to pay tithes. They were consumed with a desire to have God transform their nation.

The primary mandate for every believer is not to work at a job and come to church to pay tithes.

JESUS' REVEALS HIS PRIORITY

In Jesus' parables, He described the Kingdom of God as a mustard seed that is capable of growing up to take over the whole forest. He also said it was like leaven that leavens the whole lump of dough, leaving no piece unchanged by its pervading presence. When leaders only preach the gospel of salvation and view the church's role merely as a personal refuge for believers, a means of escape from the godlessness of the world, they malign the true gospel. They reduce the supernatural power of the Kingdom of God to transform and extend the Kingdom throughout the earth. They make God a half-God—strong enough to change a person but not powerful enough to influence and transform all of society.

Through the power of His redemption, Christ has made believers to rule as kings on the earth (Rev. 1:6). Just as a king has a political kingdom—a domain where he reigns—so Christians are destined to extend His Kingdom as they reign in this life. The life of every believer should be dedicated to reigning over their God-given territory, their personal sphere of influence. As each believer makes his priority to subdue his "promised land" according to Kingdom principles, the earth can be filled with the glory of the Lord.

Christ's ultimate purpose is for the glory of God to be restored to the whole earth. Hence, this is the significance of "Christ in you the hope of glory" (Col. 1:27). You are the hope for restoring the glory of God—His dominion and Kingdom rule— throughout the earth. That restoration of God's reign is not to be realized only in the future millennial reign of Christ, it must begin now. This is the Biblical mandate of the church—the body of Christ on the earth today. There is no more important purpose for its existence.

Throughout history, there are accounts of powerful revivals that transformed lives, communities, and entire nations. One such account is the Great Awakening of the 1730's and beyond, which began in England and swept the American Colonies. It brought people back to born-again relationship with Christ from cold, traditional religion. They experienced new levels of intimacy with God, which transcended denominations, class, and cultural status. Individuals, regardless of education, race, or position in life, were worthy of God's love and transforming power.

Powerful preachers such as Jonathan Edwards and George Whitefield, as well as John Wesley and others, were responsible for large ingathering of souls during this Awakening. Their sermons were based on true religion, which meant trusting Biblical revelation rather than human reason. In that way, the revival counteracted the strong currents of the Age of Enlightenment rampant in Europe, which had made reason supreme.

This spiritual reality, experienced in the salvation of multitudes of people, united them over political and religious divides. Some credit this revival with preparing the American colonists for their Revolution in which they gained freedom from England, by breaking the false notion that a "state church" should be honored and obeyed above God's laws of justice and liberty. Even politically, an entire nation was influenced by the gospel truths of the Kingdom preached by men and women who were totally abandoned to God. They asserted that the Kingdom was not for a few educated, religious elite, but for individual believers who are empowered and indwelt by God, Himself.

THE SOLE MISSION OF JESUS

The scriptures teach that the mission of Jesus was twofold: to redeem mankind through His death and resurrection, and to extend the Kingdom of God throughout the earth. Originally, God gave Adam the responsibility to fill the earth with God's glory. The first couple was not commanded just to multiply and fill the earth with other people. They were given the authority to subdue the earth and extend the glory they enjoyed as they walked with God. The glory of God in which they lived before they sinned was to be multiplied throughout the whole earth. His love, wisdom, power, humility, and every divine virtue were intended to characterize life on earth.

Jesus, who is called the last Adam (1 Cor. 15:45), came to restore to the earth the glorious Kingdom that the first Adam forfeited. After John was put into prison, Jesus began to preach, "The time is fulfilled, and the kingdom of God is at hand. Repent, and believe in the gospel" (Mk. 1:15NKJV). Jesus also declared, "…If I cast out demons with the finger of God, surely the kingdom of God has come upon you" (Lu. 11:20NKJV). It is important to note that the church had not been introduced when Jesus announced that the Kingdom of God, Jesus' domain, had come to earth.

It may surprise you to know that Jesus's primary assignment was not to establish the church on the earth; His primary mission was that through the church he would restore the Kingdom of God and His glory to the whole world. Jesus reflected that glory in His life on earth. He established the righteousness of God in every situation that He touched, restoring the glory of God and bringing the Kingdom of heaven to earth. And that is His intent for every believer. In His model prayer, when Jesus taught His disciples to pray, Jesus emphatically declared this Kingdom mission:

> After his manner therefore pray ye: Our Father which art in heaven, Hallowed by thy name. Thy kingdom come. Thy will be done in earth, as it is in heaven
> **—MATTHEW 6: 9–10**

> And Jesus prayed for the glory of God to fill the earth through the lives of His followers that He sends into the world:
> As thou hast sent me into the world, even so have I also sent them into the world…that they all may be one; as thou, Father, art in me, and I in thee, that they also may be one in us: that the world may believe that thou hast sent me. And the glory which thou gavest me I have given them…
> **—JOHN 17:18, 21–22**

This dual mission of Jesus, to redeem mankind through His death and resurrection and to restore the Kingdom of God on the earth has been largely misunderstood by the church. As a result, the gospel of salvation preached today is only half a gospel; it denies the reality of the destiny of Christians to restore the glory of God and extend His Kingdom principles in every sphere of life where they have influence.

Because the church is not modeling the gospel of the Kingdom, as the Biblically mandated lifestyle of believers, to take the principles of the Kingdom into their daily lives, our youth today are caught in a crisis of belief. Research among kids who regularly attend church reveals that young people who lack basic Biblical principles as a basis for their belief system are over 200 percent more likely to be angry with life, resentful, lacking purpose, and will ultimately become disappointed with life. They are also much more likely to lie to a friend, steal, physically hurt someone, use illegal drugs, and attempt suicide.

Instead of having strong beliefs in absolute truths about God, salvation, moral conduct, and other Kingdom themes that Jesus taught, church youth today are accepting "subjective" truth, i.e., what a verse of scripture means to me. These young people are hearing truth through their own filter, which tells them that all truth is personally determined. The majority of today's youth say there is no absolute moral truth. They have not believed the Kingdom truth declared by Jesus, "I am the way, the truth and the life. No one comes to the Father except through Me" (Jn. 14:6)

THE CHURCH IS NOT THE KINGDOM OF GOD

Widespread confusion regarding the mandate of the church has resulted in its failure to fulfill its primary purpose: to extend the Kingdom of God on the earth. Many erroneously believe that the church and the Kingdom are synonymous terms. Jesus demonstrated through His teachings and lifestyle that the church and the Kingdom of God, while integrally related, are not synonymous.

When Christ introduced the church, He declared: "I will build my church and the gates of hell will not prevail against it" (Matt. 16:18). His next words to the disciples were: "And I will give unto thee the keys of the kingdom of heaven" (:19). It is clear that in that discourse Jesus took the responsibility for building His church, while giving His disciples the keys of the Kingdom. He gave them the responsibility for extending the Kingdom of heaven on the earth: His righteousness, peace and joy in the Holy Ghost. So effective were those keys for the early Christians, that people exclaimed, "These that have turned the world upside down are come hither also" (Acts 17:6).

Many pastors have taken it upon themselves to "build" their church, according to their pattern, their personality, and for their purposes. For them, the church consists of   expensive facilities, lots of people and providing attractive programs. The purpose of church programs is to keep their members busy and out of trouble, keep them coming to their church, and motivate them to finance more church programs.

These pastors find it necessary to try to "control" their membership to keep them from going to another church they might find more attractive. Their churches engage in unhealthy rivalry, pastors compete instead of cooperating, striving to build the best facilities, promote the best programs and music, and to be the most popular leader. The goal is not to extend the Kingdom; the goal is to 'build my church'.

Some leaders scarcely notice the lack of power displayed in their lives and the lives of their members to bring redemptive change to their community. And, while pastors lament over the large-scale exodus from their churches, especially among younger members, they often consider it just "a sign of the times."

I wrote in my book, ChurchShift, the inevitable result of "doing church" as I have just described:

Too many Christians and Christian leaders spend their energy, creativity, and precious time promoting churches instead of the Kingdom. They work for the success of their church, or perhaps for a group of churches in their city, or they work for their ministry or denomination. They believe that by building churches and ministries they are building the Kingdom. They think church and Kingdom are practically synonymous. This isolation of the church from the world has led to ineffectiveness and failure to carry out the Great Commission.

Believers who are taught to simply attend church and be involved with the weekly programs of the church become distracted in their daily lives with worldly values and goals: earning a living, enjoying recreation, and adopting many of the mindsets of today's godless society. They don't understand that their job or career is to be more than just a means of economic stability, that they aren't supposed to just work for a living. They don't know that they are to discover their destiny to extend the Kingdom of God, its values, principles, and lifestyle into their place of employment, throughout the community and beyond.

In an article titled, "Americans Have Commitment Issues, New Survey Shows", the Barna Research group cites what they call soft Christianity, concluding:

...Americans are willing to expend some energy in religious activities such as attending church and reading the Bible, and they are willing to throw some money in the offering basket. Because of such activities, they convince themselves that they are people of genuine faith. But when it comes time to truly establishing their priorities and making a tangible commitment to knowing and loving God, and to allowing Him to change their character and lifestyle, most people stop short.

PURPOSE OF THE CHURCH

Through His apostles, Christ revealed the preciousness of the church and the power and purpose that is entrusted to it. According to the epistles, it is clear that God put all things under Christ's feet, "and gave Him to be head over all things to the church, which is His body, the fullness of Him who fills all in all" (Eph. 1:22). Husbands are admonished to love their wives "just as Christ also loved the church and gave Himself for her, that He might sanctify and cleanse her with the washing of water by the

34

word, that He might present her to Himself a glorious church, not having spot or wrinkle or any such thing, but that she should be holy and without blemish" (Eph. 5:25-27).

The apostle Paul teaches all believers that they are to give honor to each other as members of Christ's body, functioning together and living in interdependency with one another to build up the body of Christ (1 Cor. Chapter 12). And he revealed the mandate of the five key ministry gifts of the church – apostle, prophet, evangelist, pastor, and teacher for "…the equipping of the saints for the work of service, to the building up of the body of Christ…" (Eph. 4:12, NAS).

Paul explains that the primary purpose of church leadership is to equip believers to fulfill their destiny in answer to the heart cry of God for the earth: "Thy kingdom come. Thy will be done on earth as it is in heaven". And Jesus stated clearly that He had come to "seek and to save that which is lost" (Lu. 19:10). As believers are equipped for service, they will be filled with passion to do the same, to fulfill the heart cry of the Head of the church and to seek the redemption of lost souls.

Only in pursuing this clear mandate can church leaders begin to establish the Kingdom Driven Life and become the "salt and light" of the world. Any lesser path results in the church functioning as an ecclesiastical dynasty hidden within four walls, reciting empty and powerless creeds of theological dogma. These practices make the church less relevant to the lives of even sincere believers in our world today.

The purpose of every Christian is to be like leaven, influencing the environment where God places them until it is quietly transformed to reflect the glory of God. Without this understanding of priority and purpose, much of the church has become powerless to affect the spiritual and moral darkness of the society in which we live.

The church must learn to rule and reign in every area of life where believers are in order carry the glory of God into those places. They are to become God-carriers to transform their sphere of influence, extending the principles of the Kingdom there. According to sociologists, there are seven major spheres of life, which are categorized generally as follows:

1. Spiritual/Social
2. Government/Politics
3. Business/Economy
4. Education/Science
5. Media
6. Culture/Entertainment
7. Sports

The apostle Paul wrote to Timothy so that he would know how to conduct himself in the house of God, "which is the church of the living God, the pillar and ground of the truth" (1 Tim. 3:15). All of society is to feel the powerful, transforming influence of this "pillar and ground of the truth", the church. In order for the glory of God to fill all the earth, it is necessary that the truth and the principles of His Kingdom become pillars upon which all of society rests.

PRIORITY OF THE KINGDOM

Jesus articulated the priority of the Kingdom, the Father's divine heartbeat when He taught us to pray: "Thy kingdom come. Thy will be done in earth as it is in heaven" (Matt. 6:10). True disciples of Christ will be motivated with the passion of God's heart to restore His Kingdom, His will, His power, and His glory in all the earth. The godliness demonstrated in the realm of heaven must become the reality of earth. Extending the principles of the Kingdom of heaven throughout the earth, throughout all of society, is the mandate of the church—of every believer. The ministry of reconciling people personally to God, increases the number of people who carry God's glory throughout the earth.

What does this divine priority—the heartbeat of God—look like in the 21st century? It means that every believer must learn to occupy his or her "promised land", as the children of Israel were assigned to do. As they routed the beasts and the giants dwelling in the Promised Land, they possessed it, subduing it to the will of God (Ex. Chapter 23). They did not huddle together in their tribes and allow the inhabitants of the land and the beasts of the field to rule over them.

Jesus' priority of the Kingdom is missing in many churches today. Instead of the passion to establish Kingdom principles and values on the earth, we see an attitude of apathy and lack of motivation, even defeat, in many church-goers and church leaders. Church-goers and leaders have some sense of saving people from the domain of darkness but little sense of being saved to fulfill our Kingdom purposes. It is almost like people think our salvation is punctuated by a pause while we await our eternal purposes in heaven.

DEMONSTRATING THE KINGDOM OF GOD

The influence of Kingdom of God is ordained and destined to cover and impact the entire earth. It is the mustard seed that becomes the largest tree providing shelter for the birds of the air (Matt. 13:31); it is the leaven that leavens the whole lump, penetrating every sphere of society with godly principles (Matt. 13:33); it is the river of God dwelling within every believer that satisfies the lost, thirsty souls (Jn. 7:38).

As the founding pastor of the largest church in Europe, I can testify to the redemptive, transforming power of these Biblical principles for extending the Kingdom of God on the earth. Twenty one years ago I began with 7 people, and today, besides the 25,000 members in our church, over 2,000,000 souls have given their hearts to Christ at our altar. And there are about 1,000 churches that have been established through our ministry, with many reaching into other nations as well.

Our church was not established through popularity or media coverage or large endowments. On the contrary, as a young black man from Nigeria, I suffered the prejudice of race that is rampant in this country. The government accused me of being a leader of a cult, of controlling people and other absurdities. They tried to kick me out of the country; but God's will prevailed.

Jesus is building His church in our former communist nation as we dare to train and equip believers to apply the principles of the Kingdom and extend the values of the Kingdom in their sphere of influence. Our church was established through the transforming power of God that changed lives, one at a time, as we demonstrated and taught the principles of the Kingdom that Jesus taught.

Demonstrating and teaching these Kingdom principles has resulted in our church establishing over 3,000 autonomous organizations in our nation, led by members of our church with many being sponsored and not financed by the government. Believers are wielding their godly influence through practical programs accepted and sponsored throughout our city, our nation, and in other nations of the world. Our members have invaded even the political system and are serving our nation's government in a godly way to bring reforms and extend values and lifestyles based on Kingdom principles.

Do not be tempted to think that the impact we are having in our nation is a phenomenon, or that it is "God's time" just for Ukraine. I encourage you not to dismiss these testimonies as powerful examples of what is happening only within our cultural paradigm. Kingdom principles apply to the church worldwide and release their supernatural, transforming power for all believers who will embrace them.

EMPOWERING YOU

As I mentioned, according to the scriptures, the focus of church leadership (apostles, prophets, evangelists, pastors and teachers) is to equip the saints for the work of the ministry. The apostle Paul wrote:

> Their responsibility is to equip God's people to do his work and build up the church, the body of Christ, until we come to such unity in our faith and knowledge of God's Son that we will be mature and full grown in the Lord...
>
> **—EPHESIANS 4:12–13 (NLT)**

To that end, as a pastor, I have written The Kingdom Driven Life to help empower church leaders and believers alike to embrace the revelation of the Kingdom of God. The church must learn to reflect the personality of God on the earth, His nature, and His characteristics as they are witnessed in the lifestyle of believers.

Jesus did not come simply to save us from sin, but to give us abundant life (Jn. 10:10). He is not a half-God; He is absolute. He came to restore His righteous to the domain of the earth and extend the influence of His Kingly domain now, not only in His future millennial reign. He gives believers authorization to reign as kings and priests on the earth, to do greater works than He did and to fill the earth with His glory. To that end, the church must fulfill its mandate to multiply the number of believers and to equip believers to extend the Kingdom of God in the world.

Are you a pastor or leader who longs to see the Kingdom of God extended on the earth? Are you a believer who desires to do the will of God? Do you desire to fulfill your divine destiny? Are you lacking zeal and passion for the Kingdom? These life-questions must be answered honestly by every Christian leader and believer.

You may have wondered if a believer needs to receive Jesus Christ making Him pre-eminent in our life making Him Lord, embracing the Kingdom of God in our inner being before he can be regarded as saved. However on the other hand the question could be asked, "Is it possible to have brought salvation to a believer without necessarily having had made Jesus Christ our Lord without making the truth about the Kingdom of God part of us?" For the purposes of the invasion of the Kingdom of God on the earth, God in His wisdom purposefully designed our process of salvation in such a way that it requires us to receive Jesus Christ and participate in His Kingdom. He does this by making every believer to become a God carrier and a person who extends the Kingdom. The sole purpose for receiving Jesus Christ, is not just for appearance, to wear a badge of salvation, or just for fun. It is because God needed someone who would actually carry His life and reflect Him on a daily basis, revealing Him to as many as have not discovered Him. So His Kingdom assignment to us is intimately linked with our very salvation.

In the same vein, the reason we receive the Kingdom of God inside of us when we are born again is that it is an integral part of the life of any believer to not just carry the Kingdom of God, but to actually extend the Kingdom and work for its progress wherever he or she goes. However, this Kingdom aspect of our salvation and our Christian life is often neglected. Not very many believers connect their salvation to the mandate of revealing God and extending the Kingdom of God through each individual believer. This is what God wishes to restore back to the modern church today.

Some might wonder if the Kingdom of God is already within you, as I explained in the first chapter, why do we still need to receive Jesus and the Good News of His Kingdom at salvation? The importance is we need to understand that the whole creation is created according to the principles and laws of the Kingdom. The laws that govern creation and humans on the earth are in accordance with the principles and the nature of the Kingdom of God. If we don't understand the Good News of the Kingdom, we cannot convey it.

However, we individually still need to receive Jesus as our Lord and Savior, thereby receiving the regeneration of our spirits. It is that Spirit of Christ that causes our spirits to be born again. Without that Spirit, there would be no grace to live according to the laws of the Kingdom. So, even though we are created to live by love, no one would be able to live in love without the Spirit and the grace of God.

Even though man and the creation are made to function according to the laws of the Kingdom yet no one would be able to fully live by these laws without the Spirit of Christ and His grace indwelling them. However, even when a person is born again, he or she will still need to study the word of God to become consciously aware of these laws of the Kingdom by which he was created to function. In other words, even though we are created to function by the laws of the Kingdom, a person will find it difficult to be aware of that or know the laws until he renews his mind through the direct work of the Spirit or through Biblical studies that will enable the laws to come to reality in his life. At times people discover the principles of the Kingdom that work to successfully manage businesses or relationship issues or other things. We should realize that the principles work because they are the laws and principles of the Kingdom that apply to all people.

The laws and the principles of the Kingdom become effectual in our personal lives as we renew our minds with the Word of God and exercise the discipline to embrace the image of Christ. Only in this way can we effectively carry the Kingdom, His life and principles, to the outside world.

As you dare to embrace these Kingdom principles, you too will become an effective God-carrier on the earth. And the powerful, life-changing testimonies that follow will inspire even the most discouraged Christian leader and believer to believe that you too can become a powerful force to extend God's Kingdom on earth in our generation.

Chapter 1

THE PURPOSE OF THE KINGDOM

"Now when He was asked by the Pharisees when the Kingdom of God would come, He answered them and said, 'The Kingdom of God does not come with observation; nor will they say 'See here!' or 'See there!' For the Kingdom of God is within you.'"

—LUKE 17:20-21

What was the original plan—the heartbeat—of God in His work of Creation? For what purpose did He create mankind? It is clear from the scriptures that God did not create the earth because of a momentary whim or to demonstrate His great power and creative ability. He did not bring the universe into being because He was bored or for lack of something better to do. God has revealed Himself throughout the scriptures as a God of purpose, with eternal significance to everything He does. The prophet Isaiah declares this purposefulness of God:

> The LORD of hosts hath sworn, saying, Surely as I have thought, so shall it come to pass; and as I have purposed, so shall it stand…For the LORD of hosts hath purposed, and who shall disannul it?…
> **—ISAIAH 14:24, 27**

And the apostle Paul referred to God's strength of purpose, when he declared:

> …Having made known unto us the mystery of his will, according to his good pleasure which he hath purposed in himself…In whom also we have obtained an inheritance, being predestinated according to the purpose of him who worketh all things after the counsel of his own will: That we should be to the praise of his glory, who first trusted in Christ
> **—EPHESIANS 1:9, 11–12**

It is clear that God created the earth for a specific, divine purpose. He had an agenda—a specific assignment for the earth and for mankind to fulfill. His purpose as a Creator was based in a profound need resident within the Godhead. In spite of the theological argument that God is self-sufficient and has need of nothing, the astute Bible student will discover that God does have a need—one that only mankind can fulfill. The late Fuchsia Pickett, D.D., beloved Bible teacher and theologian, describes this need of God's heart that resulted in His creating mankind:

Let's allow our imaginations to take us back into the eons of eternity, to the "beginning," to listen to the triune Godhead as They expressed a deep desire among Themselves. Because of who

God is, He had a need. Though our theological understanding of God's self-existence, which pictures God as having need of nothing, often prevails in our thinking, all Scripture testifies to the contrary, showing us that God had a need. "God is love" (1 John 4). Love is not merely an attribute of God's character, but the essence of His being. The nature of love requires a recipient, one who will respond by choice to the love given. Because God is love, He needed someone to respond to His love. Because of that longing, They said among Themselves, "Let us make man in our image" (Gen. 1:26). God expressed His need in His desire for a family, one into whom He could pour His very nature. [Fuchsia Pickett, Th.D., God's Purpose for You, (Lake Mary, FL: Strang Communications, 2003), p. 7]

God created the earth for a specific, divine purpose.

God is Love, and because of the insatiable desire of divine love, He had a need. God needed creatures into whom He could pour His love-nature; who would be able to reciprocate His love. So God took a fragment of heaven—the Kingdom of God—with the heavenly realities found in the presence of God, and formed the garden of Eden. Then he created mankind—Adam and his wife—and placed them in that garden where the presence and glory of God dwelt. Mankind was originally enveloped in the pure atmosphere of divine love—the glory of God—complete with all the attributes we use to describe Love—God Himself.

IN THE BEGINNING

Adam and his wife were the first human recipients of God's love on the earth. Because they were made in the image of God, they also shared a deep, intrinsic need to love and be loved.

To maintain their well-being required that they commune with God and fellowship with Him continually, receiving His love and reciprocating that love. They were the answer to the need of God—His heartbeat—to be able to love and to be loved in return. He was their total fulfillment, their reason for living and the source of their destiny. God blessed His first couple, and gave them their assignment—their divine destiny:

> And God said, Let us make man in our image, after our likeness: and let them have dominion over the fish of the sea, and over the fowl of the air, and over the cattle, and over all the earth, and over every creeping thing that creepeth upon the earth. So God created man in his own image, in the image of God created he him; male and female created he them. And God blessed them, and God said unto them, Be fruitful and multiply, and replenish the earth, and subdue it: and have dominion over the fish of the sea, and over the fowl of the air, and over every living thing that moveth upon the earth.
>
> **—GENESIS 1:26–28**

Adam and Eve were to follow the command of God to be fruitful and multiply, to take dominion over the earth and subdue it. They were to extend the atmosphere of the Garden throughout the whole earth—the glory and presence of God and His divine order. In this way, Adam and Eve would establish the Kingdom of Love as they subdued the earth, taking dominion over every living creature. That was God's intended purpose for mankind when He created them in His image. In that sense, the garden of Eden was a prototype for God's Kingdom that was to be established throughout the whole earth. Mankind's assignment was to extend the Kingdom of Love throughout the earth.

A HEROINE OF KINGDOM LOVE

Corrie ten Boom is a familiar name to many who have studied the history of the Holocaust. She was born to a watchmaker in Amsterdam, the youngest of three sisters and one brother. They were raised in the Dutch Reformed Church. Corrie was outgoing and strong-willed. She attended Bible school for two years. She is best known for her involvement in the Dutch underground. Her family hid refugees in their own home. In 1944 she was arrested along with her entire family. They were ultimately removed to the infamous Ravensbruck prison in Germany. Corrie was released in 1945, just days after her sister Betsie died. She allowed the love of God to fill her heart with forgiveness for her captors and began to live for many years as an itinerant preacher, sharing her story of God's love and grace in over 60 countries.

Corrie was a prolific writer, and in a little devotional called, Each New Day, she explained the love of God with this simple analogy:

We must mirror God's love in the midst of a world full of hatred. A mirror does not do much. It only hangs in the right direction and reflects light. We are mirrors of God's love, so we may show Jesus by our lives. He uses us to spread the Gospel of the Kingdom and to glorify Jesus. Thank You, Lord, that by Your Holy Spirit You turn our eyes in the right direction, looking unto You, that You can make us Your mirrors. What an honor, what a joy! [Corrie ten Boom, Each New Day, (Old Tappan, New Jersey: Fleming H. Revell Company, 1972), p. 17]

Adam and Eve were to establish the Kingdom of Love as they subdued the earth.

47

From the Biblical narrative, we understand that the earth was created to function according to the principles of divine love that rule the Kingdom of heaven. Because God created the earth to be a reflection of heaven, He wanted mankind to extend the glory of His presence—His domain of love—beyond Eden. For mankind to fulfill their destiny it would mean that they would bring the whole earth under the rule and principles of His divine Kingdom. Earth would become a reflection of the heavenly order, filled with the bliss and harmony that all creatures enjoy in the glorious presence of God.

In the garden of Eden, mankind lived in the sublime reflection of the reality of heaven, communing with God and living life in a spiritual dimension that connected them to their eternal destiny. For example, through uninhibited relationship with His Creator, Adam was empowered to name the animals and to take dominion of the earth. They talked with God, hearing His voice as He walked in the garden in the cool of the day (Gen. 3:8) and learning His commands for their lives. They understood their assignment; they knew what they could and could not do in the garden.

When God told Adam and Eve to be fruitful and multiply, He was not simply referring to their giving birth to children to populate the earth, as some have taught. Pro-creation is a natural biological attribute inherent in all of God's creatures. God's original design was for them to spread out and cover the earth with His glory, His nature, in order to subdue it and establish on the earth the principles of the Kingdom of heaven. God's larger purpose for creating the earth and mankind was to make the earth a temporal reflection of heaven, filled with the glory of God.

Adam and Eve were given the earth as their domain, their place to rule over the creatures and to be lords on the earth as God is Lord over all creation. As representatives of God, Adam and Eve were given dominion for the purpose of subduing, taking responsibility for the entire earth. In that sense, the earth became the "kingdom" of Adam and Eve. Mankind was to fill the earth with the glory of God, the principles of the Kingdom of heaven, and all the attributes of divine love that rule in heaven.

The assignment of Adam and his wife was to multiply in order to populate the earth with glory-filled, Kingdom-principled men and women living in an atmosphere of heaven on earth. Eden was a place where the glory of heaven was expressed in the love of God for all His creation. Many things that make heaven to be heaven were present in the garden of Eden. It was God's intention that mankind extend heaven's reign to the whole earth.

Mankind was to fill the earth with the glory of God.

In Eden, God established His Kingdom on earth, according to its divine principles and natural laws for life. There, He gave mankind their assignment—their destiny—to subdue the earth and establish God's loving, kingly domain on the earth. From the limited area of Eden, mankind was to fill the earth with that heavenly atmosphere, lifestyle, and divine character of God's love that they shared together as they communed face to face with Him in the garden. The garden of Eden was a prototype for God's heavenly Kingdom that was to be established throughout the whole earth. Mankind's original destiny was to extend God's glorious dominion of love throughout the earth.

THE GLORY LOST

Sadly, God's original intention for mankind seemed to have been thwarted by their wrong choices. This "sovereign" power of choice—free will—was absolutely necessary to the creation of mankind. God did not want "puppets" to love Him. He desired for mankind to choose to reciprocate His love for them, for that is intrinsic to the nature of love. Love can never be required or forced; love is always, by definition, a choice.

Beguiled by the serpent into believing its lies, Eve chose to abandon her love for God, disregarding His command :

> And the woman said unto the serpent, We may eat of the fruit of the trees of the garden: But of the fruit of the tree which is in the midst of the garden, God hath said, Ye shall not eat of it, neither shall ye touch it, lest ye die. And the serpent said unto the woman, Ye shall not surely die: For God doth know that in the day ye eat thereof, then your eyes shall be opened, and ye shall be as gods, knowing good and evil.
> **—GENESIS 3:2–5**

Eve ate of the tree and Adam joined in her disobedience. When they chose to eat of the forbidden tree, disobeying the law of God, mankind forfeited their relationship with God. Filled with fear, their eyes were opened to their nakedness. And they began the lonely journey of living unto themselves without the fellowship they had enjoyed with their Creator. They lost the glory of God and the heavenly atmosphere in which they had lived.

And in a dreadful sense, like the serpent promised, they did become "as gods", exercising their independent "lordship" to rule their own lives. It meant they had to fend for themselves, without the supernatural infusion of divine love and light—the glory of God—for which they had been created and without which they could never know the fulfillment God intended.

When mankind fell, they lost that glory of God. The apostle

Paul explains: "For all have sinned and come short of the glory of God" (Rom. 3:23). This was the tragedy of their choice; they lost the presence of God in their lives when they disobeyed His command. Sin caused the glory of God to be shut out. Heaven left earth; its royal Kingdom was lost to all of mankind.

When the glory departed, Adam and Eve discovered their nakedness because the glorious presence of God no longer covered them.

All of the misery of sin down through the ages can be traced to this terrible choice that cut Adam and Eve off from their spiritual life and divine destiny in God. This terrible independence from the principles and lifestyle of divine love distorted the perspective of mankind and opened the door to the destructive power of sin. Instead of living to subdue the earth in love as God purposed, men have tried to subdue each other, by exercising lordship over people through selfishness, lust for power, greed, jealousy, wrath, hatred, murder and all malignant forms of sin. These were introduced to the earth as a result of the choice to live independently from God's Kingdom and purposes, apart from His glory. And, as they say, the rest is history.

Christians who don't know the Kingdom values cannot bring them to reign in this society. Today, even most people who attend church in America are not convinced of the absolute truth of the Bible. According to George Barna, only 9 percent of all born-again adults have a Biblical worldview. That means that less than one out of every ten Christians age eighteen or older believes that absolute moral truth exists, that it is taught in the Bible, that the Bible is accurate in its teachings and that all believers are responsible for sharing their faith in Christ with others.

When anyone lives independently of the realities and principles of the Kingdom of God, they too are "naked"—devoid of life in the spiritual dimension that brings heaven to earth. They are subjected to living a natural, soulish life, under the dominion of their darkened mind, emotions, and will. They lose the benefit of the divine connection, the relationship of their spirit with God, who is Spirit (Jn. 4:24). The scriptures compare this godless, natural existence to living in darkness, devoid of the light of God that gives meaning and significance and eternal purpose to life (Matt. 4:16).

In the garden of Eden, Adam and Eve were covered—spirit, soul and body—by the glory of God. When they sinned, that glory of the Kingdom of God was lost. It was the presence of God that made the Garden of Eden heaven on earth. That Garden was not simply a geographical entity. (Perhaps that is why no archaeologist has been able to discover it.) After all, God created the whole earth. What made Eden different from the rest of the earth was the glory of God dwelling with man.

Because of that divine presence, Eden became a physical representation of the Kingdom of heaven—a prototype of heaven on earth. When the presence of God left, there was no longer a place for the glory of heaven on earth. Mankind was thrust out of the garden to keep them from eating of the tree of life and living forever in that terrible, godless condition (Gen. 3:22–24). Adam was forced to till the ground to sustain life in their fallen state and Eve was doomed to suffer in childbirth, the most natural aspect of their original assignment to be fruitful and multiply.

LAWS OF THE KINGDOM

In spite of the fall of mankind, which resulted in a sin-filled atmosphere that covered the earth, God's governing principles—

52

His laws—remained in effect for His Creation. Since the earth was created to be a reflection of heaven, God had subjected it to certain natural laws that would allow it to function in an orderly fashion, as heaven functions. Of course, the earth is physical, unlike heaven, which exists in the spiritual realm. But without the precision of the Creator's natural laws inherent in creation, earth could not exist as it does.

These natural laws are still being discovered and defined by scientists in the realm of physics, astronomy, biology, biochemistry, and other branches of scientific study. According to a leading scientist, we cannot fathom the precision required for life to exist as we know it:

When scientists talk about the fine-tuning of the universe they are generally referring to the extraordinary balance of the fundamental laws and parameters of physics and the initial conditions of the universe. Over the past thirty years, scientists have discovered that just about everything about the basic structure of the universe is balanced on a razor's edge for life to exist. The result is a universe that has just the right conditions to sustain life. The oxygen ratio is perfect; the temperature is suitable for habitation of all forms of life; the humidity is adequate; there's a system for replenishing the air; there are systems for producing food, generating energy, and disposing of wastes.

Apart from the natural laws, there are more superior, spiritual laws inherent in human nature, which cannot be violated without destructive consequences. For example, the scriptures declare that God is Love (1 Jn. 4:16). It also declares, as we have discussed, that we are made in the Image of God (Gen. 1:26). For that reason, the deepest longing in every human heart from the moment of conception is to be loved and to express love in return.

Unfortunately, without knowing God, it is impossible to understand and experience the reality of divine love for which we are created. So, human beings in every culture search desperately to discover and experience "love" in many ways, some of which prove to be destructive to the human soul.

There are superior, spiritual laws inherent in human nature

For life to function as it was originally intended to function by God, you must choose to adhere to the spiritual principles, the same laws that govern heaven. They are imprinted upon your "DNA", recorded in the intricate pattern of every cell of your being. These inherent spiritual laws are awaiting your response to God in order to unlock their purpose and destiny for your life.

Because you are made in God's image, you cannot know ultimate fulfillment unless you choose to live a lifestyle that reflects His image in every aspect of your life—spirit, soul and body. The apostle Paul referred to this reality when he prayed:

> And the very God of peace sanctify you wholly; and I pray God your whole spirit and soul and body be preserved blameless unto the coming of our Lord Jesus Christ.
> **—1 THESSALONIANS 5:23**

Only as you choose to be restored to relationship with God through intimate relationship with Christ as your Savior can you begin to know the fulfillment and happiness God ordained for you. The purpose for Jesus, the Son of God, coming to earth was to restore you to the Kingdom of God. He clearly taught the restoration of mankind to His divine love:

As the Father hath loved me, so have I loved you:

continue ye in my love. If ye keep my commandments, ye shall abide in my love; even as I have kept my Father's commandments, and abide in his love. These things have I spoken unto you, that my joy might remain in you, and that your joy might be full. This is my commandment, that ye love one another, as I have loved you.

—JOHN 15:9–12

Without a personal commitment to the lordship of Christ and His Kingdom principles, you are vulnerable to every negative emotion and destructive mindset that results from sin. The destructive force of hatred catches many people, even born-again believers, with unforgiveness toward their family or others who they feel have offended them. They expend their emotional energy through venting these powerful, negative emotions on a daily basis. Others are filled with worry and anxiety, fear of the future, fear of failing, and countless other fears. This failure to abide by God's law of love brings about a costly price to the offender.

Medical science tells us more about how these negative emotions impact the human psyche, and even your physical health. Dr. James P. Gills, renowned ophthalmologist and prolific Christian author writes:

Our worries produce uneasiness in us that cause us to be irritable and susceptible to panic attacks. We also can be depressed, negative, critical, judgmental, domineering and controlling... Worry is a progressive disease that can ruin our lives, and even kill us. Worry depletes us and has tangible effects on our health. It may even cause us to have hypertension. It sometimes destroys our ability to fight against diseases by decreasing our natural immunity...Charles Mayo, co-founder of the Mayo Clinic, pointed out how worry affects the body. It affects the circulatory system, the heart, the glands and the nervous system, to name just a few. Mayo used to say that he never knew of anybody who died of overwork, but he did know people who died of worry.

Your entire being was created to function according to the laws of the Kingdom of God. Your brain, your circulatory system, your tissues, your heart, and all of your organs are formed in such a way that without your obedience to the principles of the Kingdom, you cannot enjoy mental, spiritual, and physical health.

UNDERSTANDING THE KINGDOM "WITHIN YOU"

The Pharisees, religious leaders of Jesus' day, demanded that Jesus tell them when the Kingdom of God would come. As usual, Jesus' response required a radical change of perspective:

> "...he answered them and said, The Kingdom of God cometh not with observation: Neither shall they say, Lo here! Or, lo there! For, behold the Kingdom of God is within you.
>
> **—LUKE 17:20–21**

Even today, many Christians are too "religious" to understand what Jesus was saying. They think He meant that for those who receive Jesus into their heart to be born again and receive salvation, the Kingdom of God has come to them. False. Not true. At the time Jesus declared that the Kingdom of God is within you, the disciples had not yet received Him as the Lord and Savior. Christ had not yet died and resurrected to become their Savior. And by the way, Jesus was not making that statement to the disciples; He was talking to the Pharisees. How could He say that the Kingdom of God was within the Pharisees, when on other occasions He rebuked them for rejecting the Kingdom and making it of no effect in their lives? (Matt. 15:6).

Jesus understood that the principles of the Kingdom of God are imprinted on the human spirit. And He knew that those laws were working, either positively or negatively, in the lives of every person on earth. When He accosted the Pharisees for being hypocrites, Jesus rebuked them for violating the principles of the Kingdom of God, rejecting the prophets and refusing to receive Him as the Messiah. He accused them of living a pretense of external righteousness, declaring that they "make clean the outside of the cup and of the platter, but within they are full of extortion and excess" (Matt. 23:25). Jesus specifically exposed their violation of the laws of the Kingdom when He declared:

> Woe unto you, scribes and Pharisees, hypocrites! For ye pay tithe of mint and anise and cumin, and have omitted the weightier matters of the law, judgment, mercy, and faith: these ought ye to have done, and not to leave the other undone…Thou blind Pharisee, cleanse first that which is within the cup and platter, that the outside of them may be clean also.
> **—MATTHEW 23:23, 26**

Because they had rejected the laws of the Kingdom—judgment, mercy, and faith—Jesus called them "serpents" and a "generation of vipers" who could not escape the damnation of hell. (Matt. 23:33). Those are the consequences every person faces who refuses to embrace the truth of the Kingdom of God and its principles. Kingdom laws cannot be broken; they do not change. They are inherent to the nature of mankind. But they can be violated, which brings negative consequences to the perpetrator.

In essence, Jesus told the Pharisees to watch His works and His lifestyle to contrast His obedience with their disobedience and disbelief in the laws of the Kingdom. The laws are the same for everyone; the result of choosing to obey or disobey them is what determines the outcome of your life. It is a known fact that everyone has a conscience that often rebukes us when we do wrong until this conscience is silenced through an incessant disobedience.

Kingdom laws cannot be broken; they do not change. But they can be violated.

For example, you may declare that you are an atheist, a communist, or believer in some other philosophy that denies the existence of God. That does not mean He does not exist. And if you determine to live in unforgiveness, believe it or not, you are violating the laws of Love programmed into your psyche and your body, and you will suffer the consequences. Even Christians who choose to allow hatred and resentment to rule in their lives will suffer the mental, emotional and sometimes physical consequences of such negative emotions.

It is the Kingdom of God within you—the Kingdom of love—that you are violating when you do not forgive or when you otherwise sin. You are born with the Kingdom laws programmed into your being; you were made to function according to the principles and order of God's Kingdom within. You cannot deny these Kingdom realities without paying the price that you will suffer as the consequence of your choices. King Solomon, the wisest man on earth, who lived hundreds of years before Jesus came, understood this spiritual reality:

Do not be wise in your own eyes; Fear the Lord and depart from evil. It will be health to your flesh, and strength to your bones.

—PROVERBS 3:7–8

Why does everyone want to fall in love? Because the Kingdom reality residing in your psyche and emotions yearn for love. God is Love and you are made in His image. Even in a fallen state, separated from God, your deepest need is to be loved and to love in return. And because God is the source of all love, your deepest longing is to find God, to be restored to His dominion, so that you can live in His domain of peace and righteousness. Jesus was declaring to the Pharisees that, no matter how they lived, they could not deny the reality of the Kingdom of God because its laws are programmed within them.

KINGDOM PURPOSE FOR A PEACEFUL SOCIETY

Consider with me what society would be like if it were established on the cardinal law of the Kingdom—love. It would be a society where no one offends, no one steals, no one kills. Everyone would be living to love and help one another, promoting absolute harmony and preferring others in humility. No one would covet what another had and contentment would reign. Marriages would be bliss and children would honor their parents. Governments would live peacefully and laws would promote the Kingdom reality. There would be no need for police, jails, armies, or other defense measures. Every citizen would live in safety and mutual prosperity would promote happiness for all citizens.

Now, consider a society that determines not to recognize

God and to promote values opposite to the Kingdom of Love. They determine to deny, and as a result violate, the laws of God's Kingdom. Such a Kingdom would be established on hatred, greed, covetousness, slander, and murderous intent to take what another has. What is the outcome?

No one will sleep. There is no safety. Why? Because a place where everyone hates everyone else creates the fear that someone will try to steal from you or kill you. In such a society of absolute hate, even eating can become a danger because food could be poisoned in order to kill you. In a society of hate no one will come out of their house for fear of the malevolent intentions of their neighbor. A society established on values contrary to the laws of God—of Love—will result in chaos and destruction. Nothing on earth can function successfully outside the laws of the Kingdom. So even the kingdoms of this world cannot function prosperously outside the Kingdom of God. Life can only flourish according to the laws of the Kingdom that God ordained and programmed into all of creation.

The media give daily accounts of violent crime happening in every local community and across America. Stories of child and youth abductions are commonplace. School and church "shootings" take the lives of innocent victims at an alarming rate. Violent crime, which includes murder, nonnegligent manslaughter, forcible rape, robbery, and aggravated assault, occurred 1,408,337 times in America in 2007, according to the FBI statistics. This disrespect for life is a direct reflection of violating the laws of the Kingdom of Love.

If a society is established on sexual freedom where all kinds of impurity and wanton lust are permitted in the name of liberty, the result will be that people will not want to marry or give birth to children. In such a society children will not be safe from the child molester; youth will not escape the rapist; incest will become the norm. Marriages will decline, because partners will be "free" to sleep with anyone. Such a libertine society will self-destruct from disease, murderous jealousy, and worse.

If you have a disagreement with your husband or wife and become angry, you can decide you will not love your spouse anymore. You can refuse to forgive. However, that choice means you violate a spiritual principle of love that is basic to maintaining your emotional, mental, and even physical health. As a result of opening the door to hatred, anger, and resentment, you will soon realize the misery of spirit, soul, and body that your refusal to love and forgive creates. Kingdom laws can be violated, but they cannot be broken. There will be consequences. Laws, by definition, do not change. Therefore, when you try to "break" a law, it will only result in you being broken.

When Jesus said, "A new commandment I give unto you, that ye love one another; as I have loved you, that ye also love one another", He was not declaring a legalistic code of conduct. He was revealing the spiritual requirement already in place for your DNA to function in optimal health, according to the established principles of His Kingdom.

The laws of the Kingdom of God are programmed within every person and must form the basis for all society if it does not want to perpetrate self-destruction upon its citizens. That is why, living in the midst of a communist society and a godless mindset, we have unashamedly proclaimed a life of holiness to the citizens of Ukraine. That is why we proclaim the demands of love and promote the principles of the Kingdom— righteousness, mercy, forgiveness, honesty, and humility—in the face of corruption, greed, lawlessness, and ungodly governmental policies. We understand and have experienced the wholeness and satisfaction of purpose and destiny that comes when we submit to the eternal principles of the Kingdom of God.

And that is why our church is enjoying such success in seeing thousands come to Christ, be transformed, and extending the Kingdom principles and lifestyle throughout our our nation and beyond. The Ukrainian government is having to recognize the superiority of the lives of these citizens who have embraced the Kingdom principles. Because of thousands of transformed lives, it is sponsoring many of our social programs that are impacting our society for good.

When we declare our stand for righteousness without fear, regardless of the perception of others, we are not inferior to their mindsets; we are superior. We have discovered the life-giving principles of the Kingdom of God that the world so desperately needs. If governments would promote these principles, instead of attempting to control sinful behavior while promoting their own lust for power, they would establish a society that would become a reflection of heaven on earth. The more its citizens conform to the law of Love, the less governing would be required.

YOU ARE "HARD-WIRED" FOR THE KINGDOM

Adam and Eve and every other person born since the beginning of creation have suffered the consequences of violating the laws of God. As I stated, disregarding the original intention of your Creator, Who is Love and in Whose Image you were made, will bring certain misery, unhappiness, and self-destruction to your life. The principles of the Kingdom of God are sealed into your moral awareness. It is impossible for anyone to live independently of the Kingdom of God and be truly happy—you cannot do it. Happiness is dependent upon choosing to function within the laws and principles of the Kingdom of God. The apostle Paul declared:

For the Kingdom of God is not meat and drink; but
righteousness, and peace, and joy in the Holy Ghost.
—ROMANS 14:17

According to Jesus, obedience to God in every aspect of life
is the only pursuit that will bring the Kingdom of God to earth
and fill your life with righteousness, peace and joy. When you
are thinking positive thoughts, responding positively in personal
relationships and living in an attitude of thanksgiving to God,
you achieve happiness and health for your spirit, soul and body.

**The principles of the Kingdom of God are sealed
into your moral awareness.**

The scriptures teach that God even created laughter as an
expression of happiness and joy, which results in health: "A
merry heart doeth good like a medicine" (Pr. 17:22). Your Creator
wired you to use the "medicine" of laughter to help maintain
your health and happiness. Experiencing His peace and joy are
necessary to your well-being.

Conversely, as I mentioned, medical science has determined
that anger, unforgiveness, resentment, envy, and other negative
emotions that the scriptures refer to as "sin" are responsible
for a plethora of medical conditions and diseases. For example,
the "ScienceDaily" published an article titled "Anger, Negative
Emotions May Trigger Stroke". And the American Family
Physician Journal published studies that reveal that negative
emotions increase coronary heart disease risk.

These and many other medical findings support the scriptural
verdict that "the wages of sin is death" (Rom. 6:23). God is
not telling you not to sin because sin offends Him or because
it makes Him feel bad when you sin. The reason God gave

commandments not to sin is that He knows what will benefit you and what will destroy you. When you sin, violating the spiritual laws the Creator established for His Kingdom, you self-destruct. Nothing functions normally apart from the principles of the Kingdom of God. That is why Jesus taught that you must seek first the Kingdom of God and His righteousness (Matt. 6:33).

SOCIETY HAS DISCOVERED SPIRITUAL PRINCIPLES

As humanity has developed during thousands of years, we have discovered—by trial and error—some of these divine principles that govern our behavior. In that regard, the human race developed a system of education to teach principles for healthy human relationships. We have seen how certain actions and attitudes elevate people to happiness, success, and peaceful relationships. And we also understand that when a man does evil, he will reap the results of his destructive behavior.

Education is an attempt, on many levels, to discover these unwritten, divine laws that govern the earth and to help us function within them for increased health and happiness. Mathematical laws and other laws of physics help us to live orderly lives within the natural limitations of the universe. All pursuit of knowledge is an attempt, consciously or unconsciously, to discover the established principles of the Kingdom of God for His creation. Throughout history, mankind has realized that violating the laws of the universe, even in ignorance, brings devastating results to the planet, to society, and to individual lives.

When Adam and Eve chose to disobey God's commands, they were doomed to live a life independent of their spiritual source— God Himself. Their sin against God's law, which resulted in the "fall of man", precluded the entire human race from righteous living. Their son, Cain, committed the first recorded murder out of envy for his brother, Abel (Gen. chapter 4). Since then, the history of mankind has become one of self-destruction that reaches to our present generation. Educational norms developed through the centuries have helped to inhibit this destructive behavior and regulate society.

As believers, we do not have to grope through life, hoping to avoid self-destruction by pursuing education alone. Though education can help us understand natural laws, and to some extent, even spiritual principles, it falls short of divine truth that will empower our spiritual lives. Remember, we were created in God's image and God is Spirit. God has given us His written Word where He reveals the principles and laws of His spiritual Kingdom. Without discovering and heeding His Kingdom laws, we will ultimately engage in self-destructive behavior, regardless of the level of our education.

RESTORING GOD'S AGENDA

In spite of the fall of man, God did not waver in His intention to reveal His love to mankind and to establish His glory througout the earth. He simply implemented, year after year, generation after generation, the plan of redemption, which culminated in sending His Son, Jesus, to purchase our salvation through His death on the cross. It is clear from the scriptures that the Godhead had known all along this terrible sacrifice would be necessary. They refer to Christ as "the Lamb slain from the foundation of the world" (Rev. 13:8).

Before mankind was created and before they fell from glory, God's plan was already initiated to redeem them and restore His glory—His Kingdom—to the earth. Adam and Eve lost the glory of God, realized they were naked, and were expelled from the garden of Eden. Hundreds of years later, the prophet would echo this eternal heartbeat of God, proclaiming the restoration of God's glory to the earth:

> For the earth shall be filled with the knowledge of the glory of the LORD, as the waters cover the sea.
> **—HABAKKUK 2:14**

The original purpose of God for mankind and all of creation will be fulfilled. The glory of the Lord—the atmosphere of heaven—will be extended througout the earth. That glory is what makes heaven unique. And it is that glory that is supposed to make the earth unique as well. Because it was lost when man fell, Jesus came to earth as the Light of the world to restore the glory of the Kingdom of heaven to the earth. I encourage you to pray this prayer with me for personal restoration of your life to the eternal purposes of God:

KINGDOM PRAYER

Heavenly Father, your eternal purpose for creation is awesome and wonderful to consider. And the ends you have gone to so that your Kingdom could be restored to earth is beyond my comprehension. I want to be a part of the restoration of your Kingdom to earth; I want to bring your will to earth. Please teach me to focus on your purpose, to discover my destiny, and to extend the principles of the Kingdom in my "promised land". Thank you for the direction you are going to give and for empowering me to fulfill the destiny you have ordained for my life. In Jesus name, I ask. Amen.

KINGDOM PRINCIPLES
FROM CHAPTER 1

1. God had an agenda—a specific assignment for the earth and for mankind to fulfill.
2. Because God is Love, He needed creatures into whom He could pour His love-nature; who would be able to reciprocate His love.
3. God's larger purpose for creating the earth and mankind was to make the earth a reflection of heaven, filled with the glory of God.
4. Sin caused the glory of God to be shut out. Heaven left earth; its royal Kingdom was lost to all of mankind
5. The laws of the Kingdom are inherent in human nature; written on your "DNA". You are hard-wired for the Kingdom of love.
6. Kingdom laws cannot be broken; they do not change. But they can be violated, which brings negative consequences to the perpetrator.
7. The laws of the Kingdom of God are programmed within every person and must form the basis for every society that does not want to perpetrate self-destruction upon its citizens.
8. Happiness is dependent upon choosing to function within the laws and principles of the Kingdom of God.

9. Medical science has determined that anger, unforgiveness, resentment, envy, and other negative emotions are responsible for a plethora of medical conditions and diseases.

10. Before mankind was created; before they fell from glory, God's plan was initiated to redeem them, fill them with His glory and through them restore His glory—His Kingdom—to the earth.

Chapter 2

PRIORITY OF THE KINGDOM

"…Thy Kingdom come. Thy will be done on earth, as it is in heaven."

—MATTHEW 6:10

When we embrace the true purpose of the Kingdom as we discussed in the first chapter, our lives as Christians will be turned upside down and inside out. Our priorities are changed, we discover our purpose for living, and our passion is ignited to live the life that God ordained for us to live. There is nothing more exciting than to see the glory of God restored to our lives and revealed through us to bring redemption to the world.

Throughout the rest of the book, I will be sharing with you the stories of some of my church members as well as other believers who have chosen to make living out the Kingdom of God their priority and passion for life. They are the reason we have the largest evangelical church in Europe and are influencing every sphere of society with the power of the gospel throughout our nation and in other nations as well. I listed in the Introduction the seven spheres of life that sociologists recognize, as follows:

1. Spiritual/Social
2. Government/Politics
3. Business/Economy
4. Education/Science
5. Media
6. Culture/Entertainment
7. Sports

The model of church that God has helped us to build in Ukraine is such that we train every member of the church to believe that he was not just sent to the world by accident. Everybody is sent here for a purpose: to accomplish and fulfill a particular mission that is designed into the person from heaven. It is now the responsibility of the local church and spiritual leaders to help that person discover what he or she was created for and then train the person to actually step out to accomplish that particular goal.

A good example is that of Alexander Korman:

REDEEMING THE SPHERE OF EDUCATION

Alexander Korman was 18 years old when he first came to our church. Raised without a father, he had deep hurts and emotional scars that needed to be healed. After he was born-again, he pursued the training classes of our church and began to be healed and strengthened in his faith. Through these teachings, this young man began to discover his personal destiny: to help other hurting people who had not been properly fathered. As he prayed and fasted, he continued to follow this new passion of his life. In his personal discovery that God had sent him to the earth to restore family values, painfully, he came to understand that part of his training for fulfilling this destiny was what he had suffered as a fatherless boy himself.

Mr. Korman went to university with the sole purpose of preparing himself through education to fulfill his destiny. He studied psychology and other appropriately related courses that would open doors for him to present the person of the King and the Kingdom principles that had transformed his life to other hurting people. He wanted to share the righteousness, peace, and joy of the Kingdom of God that he was experiencing. As he pursued his destiny, Mr. Korman began to realize that, while there were universities in Ukraine that produce fine medical doctors, lawyers, and other professionals, there was no curriculum program to teach young people how to become godly fathers and mothers—successful parents.

Throughout his educational process, Mr. Korman was motivated to develop such a curriculum to teach family values based in godly Kingdom principles. As he prayed and fasted to this end, he began to develop a team of co-workers, with one purpose—to become an answer to the national problem related to lack of family values and failure in parenting.

Upon his graduation from university, he founded the Institute of Fatherhood which is now officially recognized, staffed, and financially sponsored by the Ukrainian government. It has had such success, that the government now recommends anyone wanting to marry in Ukraine to attend this Institute, where they learn Kingdom principles of family values and how to be successful as a parent.

Korman's Institute of Fatherhood has international branches established in the United States, Canada, and in other countries. Why? Because one young man was taught that his destiny as a believer was to find his "promised land" of influence and restore the glory of God to that land. Through his passion for extending the Kingdom of God, Alexander Korman has redeemed much territory to the reign of the King in the sphere of family and education. He is training men and women to be God-carriers in establishing godly families.

Stories like Alexander's abound so much in the Embassy of God church that it is practically impossible to talk to a church member who doesn't seem to know the direction of the calling that God has given to him or her. They go to school purposefully to get educated in the areas which they feel have been revealed to them by God to take the Kingdom of God to that sphere of the world. Every believer has been taught to believe that they have a mandate from God to bring the influence of the Kingdom of God to a particular segment of the society.

What Alexander has done in this particular case is not just a social organization but a movement that has as its goal a total upheaval; a total change and turn around in the nations' families - bringing values and responsibilities to fathers and parents. It is defined as a movement because every leader like Alexander is actually required to keep on training and establishing similar ministries and outreaches through all other members who feel they have a similar burden. In the case of Alexander, his particular ministry has reached over 100,000 families. Can you imagine this kind of outreach through one church member?! What will happen if you have 10 church members like this?

The point is that there will never be enough church buildings to accommodate all the people. By equipping church members and sending them out, they could actually pastor a whole city or nation wherever they are. The greatest success of a pastor is not defined by how many people he succeeds in bringing to his building, but by how much impact he is able to create in the city and nation through the members that have been released to take the Kingdom to where the people are.

LIFE CHANGING KINGDOM PRINCIPLES

Close scrutiny of the scriptures reveals that the Kingdom was the only message Jesus preached. He began many of His parables with the words: "The Kingdom of God is like...." What then followed, was a graphic word picture to explain the nature, value, priority and lifestyle of His Father's Kingdom. Everywhere He went, Jesus taught and demonstrated the life-changing principles of the Kingdom of God.

Jesus taught and demonstrated the life-changing principles of the Kingdom of God.

For example, to the religious leader, Nicodemus, Jesus revealed the necessity of being born again to enter into the Kingdom (Jn. chapter 3). He set a little child in front of them to demonstrate the humble nature of one who would enter the Kingdom (Matt. 18:2). And He showed the powerful, penetrating influence of the Kingdom in the parable of leaven hidden in dough that soon leavens the whole lump (Matt. 13:33). Jesus revealed the supreme value of the Kingdom when he spoke of the pearl of great price, which the man sold all he had to purchase (Matt. 13:46). Following the "parable trail" reveals the essence of Jesus' teaching, His priority and purpose for coming to earth.

As we discussed earlier, when the disciples asked Jesus to teach them to pray, He taught them the ultimate priority of restoring the Kingdom. Most people can quote this "model" prayer from memory and entire books have been written to exegete its principles. I want to focus your attention especially on Jesus' words: "Thy Kingdom come. Thy will be done on earth as it is in heaven" (Matt. 6:10).

In spite of the familiarity of these words, have we understood how life changing this powerful petition can be? Do we comprehend God's priority for us to extend the Kingdom of God throughout the earth as revealed by these words? What does the answer to this powerful petition look like in the 21st century? How should the Kingdom of God be characterized and demonstrated in our world today?

When the disciples asked Jesus to teach them to pray, He revealed to them what God intended to be the passion and pursuit of their lives. Jesus taught them His motivating force for everything He was about and extended that mandate to their personal destiny as His followers. There is little evidence that the disciples understood the significance of this prayer, yet, in those words Jesus revealed the eternal heartbeat of His Heavenly Father.

This simple petition expresses the heartbeat of God from the beginning of time. The Creator of heaven and earth is filled with a longing for mankind to experience His Kingdom reality on earth in every realm of life—spirit, soul and body. Even before He created mankind in His image, God's determined purpose was to extend the Kingdom of heaven throughout the whole earth, as we discussed.

Yet, in spite of the prophets and the historical record of the entire Old Testament, God's Jewish nation did not understand His divine priority. The disciples' perspective of "kingdom" was centered largely around the dilemma of Israel's current captivity as slaves of Rome. They clung to their traditional expectations of a Messiah who would come to deliver them from their political oppression and establish His Kingdom in Israel.

Master teacher that He was, when the disciples said, "Teach us to pray", Jesus response gave them an eternal perspective of "kingdom". He introduced them to a radically different paradigm for life—the divine priority of the Kingdom of God::

> After this manner therefore pray ye: Our Father which art in heaven, Hallowed by thy name. Thy Kingdom come. Thy will be done in earth, as it is in heaven. Give us this day our daily bread. And forgive us our debts, as we forgive our debtors. And lead us not into temptation, but deliver us from evil: For thine is the Kingdom, and the power, and the glory, for ever. Amen.
>
> **—MATTHEW 6:9–13**

God's Jewish nation did not understand His divine priority for the Kingdom.

GOD'S KINGDOM DEFINED

What do you understand when you see the word kingdom? Unfortunately, there are so many different forms of government on the earth today that few people have a working knowledge of even a political "kingdom." And nations that do pattern their government after a kingdom do not reflect the heavenly vision of God's Kingdom.

A kingdom, by definition, is composed of a King and his domain over which he rules with absolute authority. The Kingdom of God, then, simply stated, refers to the domain or territory where God rules as King. Because the scriptures teach that God is Love (1 Jn. 4:8), His benevolent reign requires that the laws, principles, and lifestyle of Love be enforced over all His subjects and over the domain itself. God intended for the earth to become that domain from the beginning.

Jesus understood that His mission was to restore the Kingdom of God to earth. In His life and ministry, He embodied the character and demonstrated the deeds of His loving heavenly Father. And He lived wholly to do the will of the Father on earth:

> The Father dearly loves the Son and discloses (shows) to Him everything that He Himself does...I am able to do nothing from Myself—independently, of My own accord; but as I am taught by God and as I get His orders. [I decide as I am bidden to decide. As the voice comes to Me, so I give a decision.] Even as I hear, I judge and My judgment is right (just, righteous), because I do not seek or consult My own will—I have no desire to do what is pleasing to Myself, My own aim, My own purpose—but only the will and pleasure of the Father Who sent Me.
>
> **—JOHN 5:20,30 (AMP)**

Jesus did not have His own agenda to fulfill; He did not come to promote His own cause on the earth. His life mission pivoted on the ultimate fulfillment of His Father's will. He was the embodiment of the petition: "Thy Kingdom come. Thy will be done in earth as it is in heaven" (Matt. 6:10). The writer to the Hebrews emphasized this reality when He referred to Christ fulfilling the prophecy of the Old Testament:

...Sacrifice and offering thou wouldest not, but a body hast thou prepared me: In burnt offerings and sacrifices for sin thou hast had no pleasure. Then said I, Lo, I come (in the volume of the book it is written of me,) to do thy will, O God.

—HEBREWS 10:5—7

The teachings of Jesus reveal the nature of the Kingdom of God. They prioritize its divine laws and principles, and reveal the character and lifestyle prescribed for all who would be restored to His domain. The life of Jesus promoted the purpose of the Kingdom: to fill the whole earth with the glory of God, giving Him the pre-eminence of which He alone is worthy.

Jesus became the role model of the Kingdom priority, which is meant to characterize every believer's lifestyle. Their divine mandate is also clear from Jesus' teachings and from His High Priestly prayer: "As thou hast sent me into the world, even so have I also sent them into the world" (Jn. 17:21). Jesus prayed not only for His disciples, but for all who would believe on Him (Jn. 17:20). And after His resurrection, when Jesus breathed on His disciples, He said plainly: "Peace be unto you: as my Father hath sent me, even so send I you" (Jn. 20:22).

Jesus became the role model of the Kingdom priority.

SEEK FIRST THE KINGDOM

This message of the priority of the Kingdom will welcome the Lord Jesus back to earth at His second coming. Only those believers and churches who understand and embrace the priority of this message will continue to be relevant to the world and society in which they live. Jesus' priority must become our priority. We must learn, as Jesus taught His disciples, to seek first the Kingdom:

> Therefore take no thought, saying, What shall we eat? Or, What shall we drink? Or, Wherewithal shall we be clothed? (For after all these things do the Gentiles seek) for our heavenly Father knoweth that ye have need of all these things. But seek ye first the Kingdom of God, and his righteousness; and all these things shall be added unto you.
>
> **—MATTHEW 6:33**

Jesus revealed clearly here the character and lifestyle of a person who chooses to embrace Kingdom reality. He contrasted this life pursuit of the Kingdom and His righteousness with the material things people were pursuing—food and clothes and temporal "needs." He taught that life is more than meat and the body than raiment (:25). Then He made this astounding promised for those who choose to seek first His Kingdom: "...and all these things shall be added unto you". This promise is unfulfilled in the lives of many sincere believers today who labor relentlessly for material wealth, not understanding or embracing the priority of the Kingdom pursuit

Jesus' priority must become our priority.

In these few words, Jesus turned upside down the priorities and lifestyle of the people listening to Him. Unfortunately, not much has changed today for those listening to Jesus' words. How many Christians are spending their time, energy, and money to pursue temporal things in the same way as unbelievers do? Too many believers' perspective of life is focused on acquiring material things instead of seeking first the Kingdom of God. Unfortunately, they forfeit this divine promise to have all their temporal needs met as a result of seeking first the Kingdom of God and His righteousness.

WHY DO WE NEED TO SEEK THE KINGDOM?

Why would Jesus teach His disciples that they needed to seek the Kingdom when He was declaring that His mission on the earth was to restore people to the Kingdom of God and through them to the Kingdom of God to the earth? A simple word study shows that the Greek word for "seek" means to "desire, inquire, and require". It implies a search for something hidden. To become a part of the Kingdom of God, Jesus said you need to desire it enough to search it out.

This seeking is not as if the Kingdom of God is lost but as in discovering of its essence, complexity, totality, and entirety. Even though we are already in the Kingdom of God after salvation, we then begin to seek to discover the totality of the Kingdom essence and meaning. Moreover, we also dedicate and devote ourselves to seeking the advancement and priority of this Kingdom, God's rule in the hearts and lives of those on the earth; this preminence is above all else.

The Greek word translated "first" in the phrase "seek first the Kingdom of God" means "firstly in time, place, order, or importance". According to Jesus, desire for the Kingdom of God must take first place in your life, replacing all lesser pursuits for temporal things.

The desire of Nicodemus, a teacher in Israel, prompted him to seek Jesus out at night to ask Him about matters of the

79

Kingdom. He acknowledged that Jesus came from God because of the miracles he had witnessed at the hands of Jesus. And Jesus began to teach Nicodemus how to enter into the Kingdom of God: "Verily, verily, I say unto thee, Except a man be born again, he cannot see the Kingdom of God" (John 3:3).

To become a part of the Kingdom of God, Jesus said you need to desire it enough to search it out.

When Nicodemus did not understand, Jesus explained that a man must be born of water and of the Spirit to enter into the Kingdom of God (John 3:4–5). Jesus revealed the mystery surrounding this new birth, comparing it to the wind that we perceive but do not know from where it comes or where it goes. Patiently, Jesus engaged this religious man in conversation, until He was able to instruct him in the simplicity of receiving eternal life and entering the Kingdom:

> For God so loved the world, that he gave his only begotten Son, that whosoever believeth in him should not perish, but have everlasting life. For God sent not his Son into the world to condemn the world; but that the world through him might be saved.
>
> **—JOHN 3:16–17**

In this insightful conversation, Jesus revealed to Nicodemus His purpose for coming to earth, to reconcile mankind to God's Kingdom, promising everlasting life to all who believe in Him.

Every living soul longs, even unconsciously, to be restored to that original purpose for which we were created. In His "Sermon on the Mount", Jesus addressed the aimless pursuit of people for temporal things that do not satisfy the ache in the human heart.

He was revealing to them the answer to their deepest desire: to know God Who created them in His image, to fellowship with Him and find fulfillment in relationship with Him alone. He taught all who would listen that they could only find true satisfaction as they chose to pursue their purposes in Kingdom of God. Unfortunately the church has failed to teach the believers the paramount importance of this truth, hence leading to a confused and powerless church that's not capable of transforming our world to God's Kingdom standards.

Of the 77 million born again adults who are churched in the US, most describe "success" in life as outcomes related to professional achievement, family solidarity, physical accomplishments, or resource acquisition. Fewer than one out of ten believers mentioned descriptions that reflect their relationship with God when asked how they wanted to be known by others. A Kingdom priority and pursuit must be restored to the church, otherwise the church will become more and more irrelevant in the 21st century.

Every living soul longs to be restored to that original purpose for which we were created.

PURSUIT OF LIFE

Pursuit is natural to the human race; every person is busy pursuing something. It is as if we are programmed to be in pursuit of life, according to our agenda. But we have all missed the point, the original goal of our pursuit. The prophet Isaiah declared this plight of all of mankind: "All we like sheep have gone astray; we have turned every one to his own way" (Isa.

53:6). Shepherds know that when sheep go astray, they are in life-threatening danger. Isaiah made that declaration in the middle of his wonderful prophetic revelation of the Messiah, who would become the Great Shepherd of our souls:

> Surely he hath borne our griefs, and carried our sorrows…he was wounded for our transgressions, he was bruised for our iniquities: the chastisement of our peace was upon him; and with his stripes we are healed.
>
> **—ISAIAH 53:4–5**

Today, more than ever, people are pursuing their own thing—life according to their own personal ideas. Jesus said life is more than the temporal things we are pursuing. He prescribed single-minded pursuit of the Kingdom of God and his righteousness as the optimal lifestyle, promising that such a pursuit would result in giving you everything you need for living in this world—and in the world to come, everlasting life.

What does pursuit of the Kingdom look like in the 21st century? There are two fundamental aspects to Jesus' command to seek first the Kingdom of God:

1. The first involves seeking His righteousness, personally. It deals with the priority of embracing Kingdom principles to become Christ-like in character, motivation, attitude, and action or lifestyle.
2. The second involves establishing the Kingdom lifestyle on the earth. The life pursuit of every believer individually and every church corporately should be focused on extending the values and principles of the Kingdom of God on the earth (the Kingdom culture).

As you consider these truths of the Kingdom of God, I encourage you to prayerfully think of ways you need to change to enjoy the fulfillment of divine destiny in your personal life as well as in the corporate expression of your church life.

SEEKING HIS RIGHTEOUSNESS

Jesus introduced the principles of the Kingdom in what we call the "beatitudes". He began His teaching with: "Blessed are the poor in spirit: for theirs is the Kingdom of heaven" (Matt. 5:3). To be poor in spirit is to recognize one's need to receive help; it is an attitude of humility that is willing turn from our independent pursuits to seek the Kingdom of God. Religious traditions and selfish agendas are laid aside when we become poor in spirit. First, we humbly seek to know the life principles of the Kingdom. Then we seek to understand the values and priorities of the Kingdom.

To pursue understanding of what makes the Kingdom lifestyle work on the earth, we need to ask: What does it mean to be a Kingdom citizen today? If God is the King of His Kingdom and I am made in His image, how can I represent Him on the earth? In my culture? How do I make the values of the Kingdom my values? My priority? How do I effectively become the will of God on the earth?

Remember, the definition of Kingdom involves a King and His influence over a domain or territory. For the Kingdom of God to extend throughout the earth means that the environment and atmosphere of heaven is to be established on earth, as it is in heaven. In order to do that we must pursue relationship with the King and submit all of our life to His dominion—not just intellectually. We must embrace the principles and values of the Kingdom in our lifestyle.

SUCCESS AS A CHRISTIAN

To be successful in life, you must learn to be a carrier of the Kingdom in every life pursuit. You need to pursue the principles, qualities and virtues of the Kingdom, allowing them to be reflected in your attitudes, actions, relationships, and your sphere of influence—your "promised land".

The Kingdom of Love will be manifested in you to such an extent that people who don't seek God for themselves only need to observe your life to know what He is like. Being with you should make them desire the loving God you represent to them; you become a God-carrier. His glory is revealed through you to fill the "earth", the part you are responsible for is the part where you are.

Success as a Christian means that to become the essence of the presence of God on the earth; to become one with Him. The restoration of the Kingdom of God within you should shine forth like light in a dark world. When Philip asked Jesus, "Lord, shew us the Father, and it sufficeth us"(John 14:8), Jesus' instructed him that His life was a revelation of the Father's life: "He that hath seen me hath seen the Father...the words that I speak unto you I speak not of myself: but the Father that dwelleth in me, he doeth the works" (John 14:9–10).

The plan of God for every believer is that you be so "married" to Christ, so meshed together with Him and immersed in His love, His character, and His will that when people look at you they see the Father. Interacting with you, people don't need to wonder what love is, what forgiveness is, what kindness is—they see those characteristics expressed in your character and lifestyle as a Christian. The goal of every believer is to become a God Joni Eareckson Tada was seventeen years old when she dived into Chesapeake -carrier, a God-representative who reflects to others the nature of God: His peace, love, joy, kindness, and forgiveness. That sums up the first aspect of seeking first the Kingdom.

Joni Eareckson Tada was seventeen years old when she dived into Chesapeake Bay and broke her neck; since then she has been a quadriplegic, confined to life in a wheelchair. Yet, in her search for answers and her struggles to find God, she has given the world inspirational books and paintings (holding the brush in her teeth), as well as untold inspiration through her lectures and outreach to thousands of people facing similar challenges. She has learned to let God be God and to allow His love to flow through her in fulfilling her purpose in life. For the past 26 years, Joni has ministered to thousands of despairing individuals one-on-one and given them hope and inspired their love for God because of her personal love for God. Her face radiates the joy of the Lord and her words reveal the deep compassion she feels for hurting people. She has become a God-carrier, bringing people into the Kingdom and together extending Kingdom principles and Kingdom love throughout the earth.

The goal of every believer is to become a God-carrier.

EXTENDING HIS KINGDOM

The second aspect of seeking first the Kingdom goes beyond knowing the principles of the Kingdom and reflecting the character of the King. It involves seeking the advancement and absolute rule and dominion of King through love, peace and righteousness. It means to gain victory over the enemies of His Kingdom on the earth. Extending the Kingdom of God is a fulfillment of Habakkuk's prophecy: "For the earth shall be filled with the knowledge of the glory of the LORD, as the waters cover the sea" (Hab. 2:14).

To become the answer to the petition, "Thy Kingdom come. Thy will be done in earth..." means that Christians must be as leaven that penetrates society and changes the essence and nature of the community where they are living out their destiny. Churches are to wield their influence in society to change the ungodly environment of the community. All believers are to flourish like the mustard seed in Jesus' parable that becomes the greatest of herbs in the garden and supplies safety for the birds of the air (Matt. 13:31).

To establish the Kingdom means to pursue the victory of the Kingdom as your priority in life. That means that you recognize that you are not created to wake up everyday to go to a job, simply to make a living. The purpose of every believer is to spread the presence and glory of God's Kingdom in his or her place of employment. Every believer is destined to receive the substance of that Kingdom and to successfully extend it in their sphere of influence, extending the reign of the King into that territory.

To extend the Kingdom means to pursue the victory of the Kingdom as your priority in life

---

Understanding and embracing this pursuit of the Kingdom of God and His righteousness can bring radical change to the lives of Christians, as well as to entire churches. This Kingdom revelation will be responsible for the personal fulfillment of believers and the corporate effectiveness of the church.

THE WORD OF GOD BECOMING FLESH

The failure of the first couple to fulfill their original purpose and divine destiny did not deter the intention—the heartbeat—of

God for His world. The Word of God will be fulfilled; it cannot be denied. That is why Jesus came to earth with the priority of restoring the Kingdom of God. The apostle John revealed a wonderful perspective of Jesus as the Eternal Word:

> In the beginning was the Word, and the Word was with God, and the Word was God. The same was in the beginning with God. All things were made by him; and without him was not any thing made that was made...And the Word was made flesh, and dwelt among us, (and we beheld his glory, the glory as of the only begotten of the Father,) full of grace and truth.
>
> **—JOHN 1:1–4, 14**

It is one of the precious mysteries of the Kingdom that Jesus came to earth as the Word of God to fulfill the Word of God on the earth. Following His example as a role model, the disciples were given the authority and power to extend the presence of His glorious Kingdom in all the earth. Jesus taught His disciples that their assignment would be the same as that of the first couple—to establish the government of God and fill the whole earth with His glory.

Jesus said, in effect, to all believers, I have placed the Kingdom of God inside your heart; the glory that resided in the Garden of Eden is inside of you. Now you are supposed to be a carrier of that Kingdom, fulfilling the original command of mankind to spread that glory to all the earth, to be fruitful and multiply so that more people come under the rule of the King and to become carriers of the Kingdom, to have in every sphere of life, and establish my divine government throughout my Father's domain. In His high priestly prayer, Jesus declared:

> And the glory which thou gavest me I have given them;
> that they may be one, even as we are one: I in them,
> and thou in me, that they may be made perfect in one;
> and that the world may know that thou hast sent me,
> and hast loved them, as thou has loved me.
>
> **—JOHN 17:22–23 (EMPHASIS MINE)**

The vision of God for you, as a man or woman who is made in His image, is to get to know God and submit your life completely to His dominion—to the King and His Kingdom. When you are born again you become a citizen of the Kingdom of God. Your spirit comes alive to God and you are reconciled to relationship with Him.

Then, as you receive revelation of the Word of God, your thinking will be transformed and you begin to experience the passion and heartbeat of God for the restoration of His Kingdom. As a believer, you begin to be the "Word made flesh". The life of Christ within you gives you divine purpose for living. That mandate becomes the priority of your life as you learn to walk in His principles and reflect His character, His nature, in every aspect of your lifestyle. You long to fulfill the prayer of the apostle Paul:

> I beseech you therefore, brethren, by the mercies of
> God, that ye present your bodies a living sacrifice,
> holy, acceptable unto God, which is your reasonable
> service. And be not conformed to this world: but be
> ye transformed by the renewing of your mind, that
> ye may prove what is that good, and acceptable, and
> perfect, will of God.
>
> **—ROMANS 12:1–2**

As a believer, you begin to be the "Word made flesh".

The priority of the Kingdom of God must be understood from the perspective of the Creator God, Who had a wonderful plan for creating the earth and placing mankind on the earth. His plan will be fulfilled on the earth. Jesus made it plain that His mission was to implement that plan through redemption, which He alone could make possible.

But, the restoration of His Kingdom is not simply to enable mankind to be redeemed from sin and go to heaven. To understand God's original purpose for creation and its restoration through Christ, you must begin to feel the heartbeat of God. You need to feel the passion of His divine purpose for creating mankind in His image. Then, you will feel the love of the Savior as He taught the realities of the Kingdom in parables that the people could understand.

KINGDOM PRAYER

Father, in the name of Jesus, I come to thank you for saving me and allowing me to be born into your Kingdom of life. I believe You want to impact my life as I read this book and change me forever. Now, Spirit of the Lord, I pray that you would give me a special revelation and a special encounter with You as I read this message of the Kingdom Driven Life. Don't leave me the way you found me; transform me and cause me to be a world-changer for You. Lord, cause me to see my relevance and believe that I am an agent of God on the earth. Help me to believe that empowered by you I am the hope of the world and that through me You want to do great things. Father, transform my mind and my traditional, religious way of thinking. Change me. Help me to be more in love with You than ever before, to be addicted to You, so that Your love in me will "contaminate" everyone with whom I come in contact. Thank you, Lord, for the answer to my prayer. In Jesus name I pray, amen.

KINGDOM PRINCIPLES
FROM CHAPTER 2

1. The Kingdom of God, simply stated, refers to the domain or territory where God rules as King.
2. Everywhere He went, Jesus taught and demonstrated the life-changing principles of the Kingdom of God.
3. Only those believers and churches who understand and embrace the priority of the Kingdom message will continue to be relevant to the world and society in which they live.
4. Too many believers' perspective of life is focused on acquiring material things instead of seeking first the Kingdom of God.
5. The first fundamental aspect of seeking first the Kingdom of God involves seeking His righteousness.
6. The second involves establishing the Kingdom lifestyle on the earth.
7. The goal of every believer is to become a God-carrier, a God-representative who reflects to others the nature of God.
8. Christians must be as leaven that penetrates society and changes the essence and nature of the community where they are living out their destiny.

9. Jesus taught His disciples that their assignment would be the same as that of the first couple—to establish the government of God and fill the whole earth with His glory.

10. As you receive revelation of the Word of God, your thinking will be transformed and you will begin to experience the passion and heartbeat of God for the restoration of His Kingdom. As a believer, you will begin to be the "Word made flesh".

Chapter 3

PARABLES OF THE KINGDOM

"All these things spake Jesus unto the multitude in parables; and without a parable spake he not unto them."

—MATTHEW 13:34

J esus demonstrated the reality of the Kingdom of God through His teachings as well as His lifestyle. He revealed to His listeners the supreme value of the Kingdom, explained the cost and requirements to enter the Kingdom, and exposed the enemies of the Kingdom—largely through His Kingdom parables. His stories illustrated the nature of the Kingdom, revealing the King's generosity and benevolent kindness to those who would seek the Kingdom. Jesus also told parables to denounce those who were too religious to enter the Kingdom and who hindered others from entering.

Jesus preached the message of the Kingdom to anyone who

would listen: His disciples, who followed Him; the multitudes who heard Him gladly; and the religious leaders who hated Him. As you study the life and teaching of Jesus, it is clear that extending His Father's Kingdom was the ultimate priority and purpose of Jesus' life. The driving force, the passion for everything Jesus said and did during His lifetime was to restore the Kingdom of God.

Yet, the disciples did not easily understand His Kingdom message neither did the multitudes who heard Him teach. Even the religious leaders of that day failed to grasp the truth of His Kingdom message. When Jesus revealed to them the Kingdom lifestyle, it often seemed contrary to the law of God they had been taught. For example, His admonition to love your enemies cut across the "eye for an eye, tooth for a tooth" retribution of the Mosaic Law. They equated this with justice and righteousness. These religious leaders were offended when Jesus healed on the Sabbath, which to them was an obvious violation of the Mosaic Law.

In many ways, the laws and principles of the Kingdom that Jesus taught did not remotely resemble the religious lifestyle of the day. These teachings trampled on the accepted norms of the religious traditions and culture. The religious leaders fumed with anger against Jesus and the Kingdom message, yet the multitudes marveled at His words and stood in awe of His miracles. Many acknowledged that He must have come from God because of the miracles they witnessed.

Religious leaders fumed with anger against Jesus and the Kingdom message

Still, it seems even they could not grasp the significance of His teaching regarding the Kingdom of God. They declared that He taught as one with authority (Matt. 7:29). But the truth of the Kingdom principles Jesus taught sounded strange to their ears. Even Jesus' disciples, who walked with Him during His entire ministry on earth, did not seem to "get it" when He taught them that He was restoring the Kingdom of God. Their lack of understanding of the Kingdom reality seems fairly consistent throughout the narrative of the scriptures.

Yet, Jesus relentlessly preached only the Kingdom of God and its extension throughout the earth. Using word pictures that the common person could relate to, His parables often began with: "The Kingdom of God is…". He portrayed in ordinary "picture" language the extraordinary nature, benefits, value, power, and priority of the Father's Kingdom that He was establishing on the earth.

Brad Young, author of Parables: Jewish Tradition and Christian Interpretation, gives us some interesting insight into the nature of Jesus' parables:

> The reality of God is revealed in the word-pictures of a parable. Jesus and the rabbis of old taught about God by using concrete illustrations that reach the heart through the imagination. They challenged the mind on the highest intellectual level by using simple stories that made common sense out of the complexities of religious faith and human experience. On the one hand, the infinite terms that describe God are beyond human comprehension, but on the other, his infinite majesty may be captured in vivid stories of daily life.

The Greek word for parable is parabole, and means "a comparison or analogy". Young explains, "The dramatic image of a story illustration is thrown out as a comparison of the reality of the source with its fictional representation in words. It may refer to a saying or story example...Jesus of the Synoptic Gospels loves to use miniature plays to communicate his message. The word-picture of the parable creates a drama that describes in clear terms the reality being illustrated".

In His parables, Jesus compared and contrasted the realities of the Kingdom of God with the common pursuits of mankind in every sphere of life, including relationships, economics, standards of righteousness, love and forgiveness, mercy and justice. For example, He taught the transforming power of the Kingdom through the picture of leaven that transforms dough or a grain of wheat falling to the ground to die in order to bear much fruit. And He illustrated the nature of the Kingdom, which is love and true humility, with a story about a "Good Samaritan".

ILLUSTRATIONS OF THE KINGDOM

On another occasion, when the disciples asked Jesus who was the greatest in the Kingdom, Jesus took a little child and used him as His object lesson to respond to their question:

> Verily I say unto you, except ye be converted, and become as little children, ye shall not enter into the kingdom of heaven. Whosoever therefore shall humble himself as this little child, the same is greatest in the kingdom of heaven.
>
> **—MATTHEW 18:2–4**

In contrast to the humility characterized by a little child, the Pharisees and religious leaders were known for lording it over the common people and considering themselves superior to others. Jesus pronounced woe upon them for this proud, "I will ascend" attitude attributed to Satan Himself (Isa. 14:14). He declared:

"Woe unto you, Pharisees! For ye love the uppermost seats in the synagogues, and greetings in the markets" (Luke 11:43).

Of course, the Kingdom of God is supremely characterized by love; the scriptures declare that God is love (1 John 4:8). When the lawyer (an expert in the Mosaic Law) tested Jesus with the question, "Master, what shall I do to inherit eternal life?" Jesus asked him to answer his own question from his knowledge of the law. The lawyer was able to respond correctly, saying, "Thou shalt love the Lord thy God with all thy heart, and with all thy soul, and with all thy strength, and with all thy mind; and thy neighbor as thyself" (Luke 10:27). Jesus assured him that he had given the right answer.

But the lawyer, evidently feeling foolish and wanting to justify his question, feigned confusion about who his neighbor was (v. 29). To answer him, Jesus told the story of the good Samaritan who helped the wounded man on the road to Jericho, citing the failure of the priest and the Levite to stop and help this unfortunate man. Of course, the Samaritan, who was considered an outcast of Jewish society, proved to be the neighbor to the wounded man, exhibiting the love and generosity that the religious men failed to demonstrate.

Through these vivid dramas of life, Jesus continually revealed the nature of His Father's Kingdom. He taught the love of the Father, His humility, generosity, kindness and mercy. He also addressed the Father's lack of regard for unloving religious attitudes.

On one occasion, when Jesus was teaching the priority of seeking first the Kingdom of God, He reassured His disciples, saying, "Fear not, little flock; for it is your Father's good pleasure to give you the kingdom" (Luke 12:32). Notice what the Father's pleasure is – to give the Kingdom to His children. Understanding the revelation of the Kingdom and living it is God's ultimate pleasure for us Christians. It must become our ultimate desire and pursuit in life.

Through vivid dramas, Jesus revealed the nature of His Father's Kingdom.

THE PERMEATING POWER OF THE KINGDOM

The kingdom of heaven is like unto leaven, which a woman took, and hid in three measures of meal, till the whole was leavened.

—MATTHEW 13:33

Leaven is a substance that causes the fermentation of dough in bread, affecting a change to every molecule of the dough. Yeast, a common leaven used in bread, forms a carbon dioxide gas, which bubbles through and lightens and expands the batter or dough while it is baking. It is a single-celled organism that changes the texture of a lump of dough and makes it rise when baking.

Jesus described the Kingdom of heaven using the analogy of this common ingredient, leaven or yeast, a single-celled organism, that has the power to transform the entire substance in which it is hidden. As a believer, Jesus taught that the Kingdom of heaven is first of all within you (Luke 17:21), working like leaven to transform your nature so that it reflects the character of God. That same Kingdom must transform your environment, society and sphere of influence.

That divine nature of God within you is supposed to work like leaven in your sphere of influence, causing you to affect the atmosphere and environment where you are in such a powerful way that you subdue it to reflect the atmosphere of the King's domain. In this way you become the answer to the petition: "Thy kingdom come. Thy will be done in earth as it is in heaven" (Matt. 6:10).

The divine nature of God within you is supposed to work like leaven in your sphere of influence.

When you are born again into His Kingdom, you are empowered to invite others to come under his rule and to extend His principles of love, kindness, forgiveness, integrity, and all the nature of His Kingdom into every sphere where you have influence. You are to grow and mature in your relationship with Christ until you permeate society with the loving nature of the Kingdom, like the leaven that leavened the whole lump.

As I have mentioned, your focus and motivation cannot be simply to wake up in the morning to go to work and make money and pay tithes to your church. I tell the businessmen in my church that they must enlarge their vision to embrace the Kingdom purpose for their businesses. You don't work to get money. To make the Kingdom of God a priority, as Jesus taught, you must view your job as the sphere of influence where you are called to welcome people into the Kingdom and to extend the principles and lifestyle of the Kingdom.

What is the Biblical definition of a calling? It is your purpose and destiny, the reason for your existence. The apostle Paul begged the believers to fulfill their calling in God:

> I, therefore, the prisoner of the Lord, beseech you to walk worthy of the calling with which you were called, with all lowliness and gentleness, with longsuffering,

> bearing with one another in love, endeavoring to keep
> the unity of the Spirit in the bond of peace.
>   **—EPHESIANS 4:1–3**

As I wrote earlier, from the beginning God created mankind to spread His glory and subdue the earth, taking responsibility to bring people into the Kingdom and to together extend the principles and lifestyle of the Kingdom. God created you specifically to bring His Kingdom into a particular arena of life—to subdue your "promised land". After the children of Israel were given entrance, supernaturally, into the promised land their assignment was to fight the giants of the land and rout out the beasts of the field, little by little, until the land was subdued and filled with the glory of God. Though the "giants" and "beasts" of the land are different, that assignment is the same for believers today.

If you are not fulfilling your Kingdom assignment, ask God about your job to see if you are positioned where God wants you to extend his domain. Are you pursuing your vision and mission in life to fulfill your calling to extend the Kingdom? If you are, then make sure you are motivated to pursue the values and principles of the Kingdom and to extend the lordship of God over the sphere of influence He has given you.

That means your goal is to be the best employer or the best worker in your company because your goal is to promote God and His dominion first of all. And you are not doing your job primarily to get paid. Your salary is a mere compensation for your work, not the motivation for working. The value of the workplace is calculated by how great an opportunity it gives you to "leaven" that sphere of life with the divine nature of the Kingdom of God.

Your salary is a mere compensation for your work, not the motivation for working.

Many well meaning believers so often naively think that their job is automatically their calling and where they are supposed to promote the Kingdom of God. However, I must differentiate between a person's calling and their work place.

Your work place is where you are employed to do a certain work for a salary. Even though as believers we need to do our best and render the best services wherever we find ourselves, the truth is that our job or work place is not necessarily our place of calling.

Our calling is the thing that God has supernaturally built into us; or better still, it is the mission that God has committed to us before the beginning of our lives. That does not necessarily correspond with our job or even our profession. For this reason, it is essential that we seek the face of the Lord about what He has called us to do, and the place He has called us to in particular. There are ways we can discover what God has created us for and called us to do. I speak more about this in my book, Churchshift, which discusses the need of the church to equip believers to discover their mission for life. (Please see bibliography).

In the example of Alexander Korman, which we read earlier, we learned how he specifically asked God for His divine direction for his life. That is what I teach all believers to do in my church.

There are so many things that can distract us while we are seeking our personal mission for life, especially attractive salary proposals or prestige of position. However, a man who is conscious of his divine calling will not be distracted or waver because of money, peer pressure or parental influence in choosing a particular profession.

The only legitimate influence that must be considered before choosing a profession ought to be the leading of God and the calling He has given us from our mother's womb.

Is your vision and mission in life to fulfill you calling?

PRECIOUS VALUE OF THE KINGDOM

In His parables, Jesus revealed the true worth of life in the Kingdom of God and the passion with which we should pursue it:

> The kingdom of heaven is like treasure hidden in a field. When a man found it, he hid it again, and then in his joy went and sold all he had and bought that field. Again, the kingdom of heaven is like a merchant looking for fine pearls. 46 When he found one of great value, he went away and sold everything he had and bought it.
>
> **—MATTHEW 13:44–46 NIV**

Many teach that to seek first the Kingdom and serve God effectively you need to resign your job and become a full-time worker in the church or on the mission field. That is not Biblical. There were no churches, no youth ministries, missionaries, or worship leaders when Jesus was teaching His message of restoring the Kingdom to the earth. He simply sent the twelve disciples out to teach the principles of God's Kingdom of love, to heal the sick, release captives, and to reveal the lifestyle of the Kingdom to a darkened world. Then He sent out seventy others to do the same, with great success:

After these things, the LORD appointed other seventy also, and sent them two and two before his face into every city and place, whither he himself would come. Therefore said he unto them…and heal the sick that are therein, and say unto them, The kingdom of God is come nigh unto you.

—LUKE 10:1–2, 9

It important to note, Jesus sent seventy messengers to go into the cities where He was going to follow. They were empowered to bring healing and commanded to declare that the Kingdom of God is near. When you go into your personal sphere of life, you are taking Jesus with you; He is there for one purpose— to establish the Kingdom in that place. You must believe Jesus' teaching that the Kingdom of God is within you. Then you can serve God anywhere with this Kingdom mindset. You only need to know who you are called to be and what particular assignment is given you.

When you go into your personal sphere of life, you are taking Jesus with you.

YOUR PRECIOUS TREASURE

You need to appreciate the precious treasure that the Kingdom represents. How would you answer the question: Are you willing to sell all that you have and buy your "field" in order to subdue your promised land, extend the reign of the King and bring the will of God to that "earth"? What do you value more than the

Kingdom of God's love? Where do you look for fulfillment and satisfaction? What is your passion in life?

Do you think God created you, putting all His resources within you—your brain, intelligence, physique, heart, eyes, and voice—simply for you to make money? Absolutely not! He did not intend for you to become a slave of money. The Bible teaches that the love of money is the root of all evil (1 Tim. 6:10). Money is not evil; but the love of money promotes all kinds of evil.

What is money? Paper bills made from trees, which are part of God's creation. Their value depends on man-made governments that rule societies imperfectly and with selfish motives. God did not call you to be a slave to human institutions. He put His divine resources in you to enable you to serve the Creator, not the creation. The amazing value that God places on mankind has not been understood, even by Christians. The psalmist asks some rhetorical questions regarding the high value God placed on mankind:

> When I consider thy heavens, the work of thy fingers, the moon and the stars, which thou hast ordained; What is man, that thou art mindful of him? And the son of man, that thou visitest him? For thou hast made him a little lower than the angels, and hast crowned him with glory and honour. Thou madest him to have dominion over the works of thy hands; thou hast put all things under his feet...O LORD our Lord, how excellent is thy name in all the earth!
> **—PSALM 8:4—6, 9**

When you seek the Kingdom, you begin to understand your great worth to your heavenly Father. As you relate to His thoughts of you, your eyes are opened to the destiny with which

He has entrusted you. King David understood that the purpose of mankind was "to have over the works of thy hands". Your destiny involves much more than working at a job, serving a company or accumulating "things." You are supposed to extend God's authority over creation, to rule over God's creation through the power of love, and cause it to come into alignment with the will of God.

When you seek the Kingdom, you begin to understand your great worth to your heavenly Father.

Unfortunately, many well-meaning Christians and Christian leaders forfeit their eternal destiny to impact their sphere of influence with God's character, nature, and lifestyle. They deny God's glory and His honor and choose to serve lesser creatures or temporal material values. In that way, they reduce God to their temporal concerns instead of subduing the earth to His benevolent Kingship. As a born again believer, you are destined to reflect His glory and subdue the earth, bringing it back to His domain. You are a member of His body in the world to bring people into his Kingdom and together to establish His values, His principles, His lordship over all His creation – to extend His dominion on the earth.

ADDICTED TO THE KINGDOM

I challenge you to study the parables of Jesus to develop His passion for the Kingdom. Jesus said that when a person chooses to put the Kingdom first—its values, principles, and lifestyle—to that person—everything else shall be added. That is what I call "Kingdom addiction." When God finds a person who will abandon themselves fearlessly, with all their resources, intelligence, and strength, to advance the Kingdom of God, He will respond by throwing all the weight and authority of His Kingdom behind them to extend the Kingdom through them.

When Jesus said to seek first the Kingdom, He was saying to let your education, your motivation, and your passion reflect His heartbeat: to subdue the people and systems across the whole earth to His supremacy—the benevolent rule of God over everything on earth. In a world filled with destructive addictions, God wants you to become addicted to the advancement of the Kingdom of God. Let His Kingdom be your primary, your only pursuit.

Zach Johnson is a professional golfer with the rare distinction of winning the Master's golf Tournament in 2007 over arguably the greatest golfer in the world, Tiger Woods. In his interview following his stunning victory in the most prestigious of golf tournaments, Zach said all the proper "thank you's and then expressed his gratitude to God. He said, "I felt like there was certainly another power that was walking with me and guiding me."

Zach belongs to an organization called Fellowship of Christian Athletes (FCA), which has chapters in all 50 states. These Christian athletes minister on dozens of college campuses and in more than 7,000 schools, not including summer camps, coaches' seminars, and various team prayer "huddles." The goal of FCA is to help athletes become acquainted with "God's game plan" and to have a personal faith in Jesus Christ.

Zach said that golf is really his ministry, in an exclusive interview with Sports Spectrum magazine. Before his victory at the Master's Tournament, Zach said that he had always had a platform for Jesus; "Now I just have a bigger platform".

God wants you to become addicted to the advancement of the Kingdom of God.

When you become obsessed with seeing the victory of the Kingdom on the earth; when you are caught up with advancing the Kingdom; when you dedicate your whole mind to it, you are seeking the Kingdom first. When the only thing you are breathing and eating is your desire to see the Kingdom of God advanced; when every strategy you are implementing is to see God advance in those areas of life that He has committed into your hands—you are seeking the Kingdom first. Your supreme goal is for the advancement of God's domain and rule, His success, His victory. You are passionate about it. It is that single-mindedness that makes you one with who Jesus is. And to that person—"all these things shall be added." That is the promise of Jesus to all who seek the Kingdom first.

KINGDOM FOOD

On one occasion, when the disciples left Jesus sitting by a well while they went into the city to buy food, a woman came to the well to draw water. Jesus revealed the way of salvation to her and she brought her whole town to hear Jesus. When the disciples returned with food, they offered it to Jesus and said "Master, eat" (Jn 4:31). But Jesus response surprised them. He said, "I have meat to eat that ye know not of". They wondered if someone else had brought Him food. So Jesus clarified His statement: "My meat is to do the will of him that sent me, and to finish his work" (:34).

Jesus said in essence, I have a passion; I have a mission; I am pursuing something that you cannot imagine. The Kingdom is my food, my drink, and my life. The advancement of that Kingdom, the growth and success of that Kingdom was His very breath. The Kingdom was what He lived, and ultimately died, to restore us to and through us to restore the Kingdom throughout the earth. And He is looking for Christians who are addicted to and obsessed by their desire for the supremacy and reign of the Kingdom of God.

As a Christian, you are not just the recipient of salvation to make it possible to escape hell. You must live for something greater than yourself. You must learn to live for an eternal purpose—not for the temporal present. If your goal is simply to be a good father or mother, to raise a family or to make money and acquire things, what happens when you have accomplished your goals? You are made for a much greater destiny than that— you are made for the glory of the Kingdom. With this eternal perspective, you will approach every vocation and relationship with one purpose: to extend the principles and lifestyle of God on the earth.

When that transformation occurs in your spirit and mind, the reason for your education becomes preparation for you to extend the Kingdom of God in that sphere of life. You are passionate to become the best worker, the best businessman, the best musician, the best pastor—not for wealth or fame or position, but to demonstrate the character of God in the world.

REDEEMING THE SPHERE OF THE ARTS

As we said before, every member of the Embassy of God is encouraged to discover his talent, calling or ministry. They are taught that everybody is created unique and carries a unique gift that is particular to him or her. Talent that is implanted within them will facilitate the fulfillment of his or her peculiar calling.

One of the young boys who was coming to our church, but who was infatuated with the pop world was Vadim. He had been coming to the church with his parents but his life almost became a replica of so many lives of teenagers who don't find fulfillment in the church because of their love for pop music. However, Vadim was exposed to the teaching that Kingdom principles must be brought into every sphere of life, including the so-called "jungles" of pop music. Furthermore, we taught that no matter how dark and evil this sphere of life is, we as believers are called to go and shine the light of the Kingdom of God there, rather than running away from it.

Vadim all of a sudden discovered that nightclubs and casinos could become his platform and arena for the Kingom of God, rather than the casket of evil as many view it. So he started developing his skills in the sphere of pop music, until he became the most popular and highly paid entertainer in the country. Performing in Ukraine's nightclubs and casinos, he became famous and is known by the name of "DJ Light", because of the Kingdom principles he stands for.

Today DJ Light has an enormous influence upon the youth of Ukraine that no pastor or church worker could have. He has become a role model and picture of light in the darkness by constantly advocating against smoking, drinking, drugs and sexual promiscuity. Vadim commands such respect and authority in the darkest places of our nation because he has dared to believe in his gift and the purpose God has given him. Even more importantly, he has dared to believe that God within him is the Light of the world and is greater than any darkness out there.

This is a complete departure from the attitude of many Christians who discourage their children from what they consider as evil, thereby making them avoid places like casinos and discotheques. Instead, we should expose them to the weaknesses of those places and impress on them the strength of the believer to subdue and overcome the very evil in them.

Vadim is using his God-given talents to appeal to the youth of Ukraine through the voice of radio. Eventually, after much hard work, he became the top deejay in Ukraine. He is using this fame and notoriety to redeem his promised land—the entertainment world—for the Lord. He uses his national "platform" to influence people to accept Kingdom principles. Because of his influence in the world of music, he can speak on other issues that promote Kingdom values and extend that influence to thousands of youth.

Let me emphasize that Vadim does not just "work for a living." But with his personal income and talent, he is able to help promote and extend Kingdom initiatives. His passion is to see people come into the Kingdom and to extend the values and principles of the Kingdom, and God has given him a "voice" in the nation to "preach" the gospel.

I recently heard the story of Paul David Hewson, better known as Bono. He is a famous Irish singer and musician and a well-known philanthropist. His list of honors includes Time Magazine's "100 Most Influential People" and an honorary knighthood granted by Queen Elizabeth II of the United Kingdom. He is the only person to have been nominated for an Academy Award, Golden Globe, Grammy and Nobel Peace Prize. Bono had a Christian background, but because of the heartless religious attitude around him, he was discouraged and even left the faith for some time. However, new-breed Christians with Kingdom perspective began to tell him that he could actually use his radio music to expand the values of the Kingdom. He accepted their advice. I listened to his last record release and found it to be the most Christian message by such a high profile secular artist. Moreover, because of his platform, he is able to take the Kingdom message to places few Christians will ever penetrate

PLATFORMS OF THE KINGDOM

The true motivation for every life pursuit—student, businessman, pastor, employee, mother, father,—is to extend the domain of God to rule and reign in the lives of people, together extending His glory throughout the earth. Life pursuits become platforms—"pulpits"—from which to declare Kingdom principles and demonstrate the Kingdom lifestyle of a man or woman restored to the Kingdom of God.

Jesus did not hesitate to explain the requirements for following Him and extending the Kingdom of God on the earth. He painted a very different picture from what the religious leaders of the day demonstrated by their lifestyle of arrogant pomp and hypocritical religious activities: "And from the days of John the Baptist until now the kingdom of heaven suffereth violence, and the violent take it by force" (Matt. 11:12). Passion for and pursuit of Heaven's priority will mark the true believer.

In addition to understanding the value and benefits of the Kingdom, Jesus made it plain that there were costs involved in becoming a part of it:

> If any man will come after me, let him deny himself, and take up his cross daily, and follow me. For whosoever will save his life shall lose it: but whosoever will lose his life for my sake, the same shall save it. For what is a man advantaged, if he gain the whole world and lose himself, or be cast away?
>
> **—LUKE 9:23–25**

There is personal cost involved in pursuing your platform for getting people to the Kingdom and together restoring the

Kingdom of God to the earth. But the reward, when you choose to die to your selfish agenda and follow Christ wholeheartedly, far exceeds the cost. When you seek first the Kingdom of God, He will throw all His weight and authority, all of His divine resources and His power behind you. When you give your strength to extend the Kingdom you will find fulfillment in life that God intended. Jesus' promise becomes yours: "...I am come they might have life, and that they might have it more abundantly" (Jn. 10:10). When you commit yourself to the Kingdom, the King commits Himself to you and you gain everything.

When you commit yourself to the Kingdom, the Kingdom commits itself to you and you gain everything.

That is why Jesus said not to be anxious about food and clothing or anything else. He is explaining that He did not create you or put all His resources in you so that you would strive and work and be anxious about what you are going to eat. He didn't create you to work all your life to make money for a living. He created you to promote the principles and lifestyle of Love. He created you to know Him and to learn that He is your life. And when you commit yourself to seeking the advancement of His Kingdom, the King will commit Himself to taking care of all your needs.

If a man or woman would be totally committed to seek the advancement and increase of the Kingdom, you would never need to worry about what to wear or eat—the King takes responsibility for you. You are His subject, His son or daughter. The entire resources of heaven are at the disposal of a man or woman who is totally committed to the advancement of the Kingdom.

When the God of heaven finds people who will honor Him through total commitment, the God of heaven will go to great lengths to honor them. Such a people will speak and heaven will stand at attention to give them the desires of their hearts because they are totally abandoned to the desires of God—the advancement of the Kingdom of God. The honor and dignity of the Kingdom of God becomes theirs. And in that exchange of losing your life to save it, the thing that was supposed to be your disadvantage turns to your supreme advantage.

When you totally surrender to promoting and extending the Kingdom, you reflect the glory and significance of the Kingdom—the hosts of heaven know your name. The angels and the Spirit of God will bypass millions of people to honor a man or woman who throws aside all of their own purposes to promote the extension of the Kingdom of God. That is the addition of seeking the Kingdom first: "all these things shall be added unto you" (Matt. 6:33).

Everything is added to the man who gives His strength to seek the Kingdom, who commits his wisdom, opportunities, and all his energies to seek the promotion of the Kingdom. In turn, God gives Him everything He has—all the silver and gold, the honor and favor of the Lord. Again, King Solomon understood the value of seeking wisdom (Who is Christ) above all else:

> I wisdom dwell with prudence...By me kings reign, and princes decree justice. By me princes rule, and nobles, even all the judges of the earth. I love them that love me; and those that seek me early shall find me. Riches and honour are with me; yea, durable riches and righteousness. My fruit is better than gold, yea, than fine gold; and my revenue than choice silver... Blessed is the man that heareth me, watching daily at my gates, waiting at the posts of my doors. For whoso findeth me findeth life, and shall obtain favour of the LORD.
>
> **—PROVERBS 8:12, 15–9, 34–35**

113

The New Testament epistles teach that Christ is our wisdom (1 Cor. 1:30). When you choose to lose your life for His sake, you will find all the treasures of wisdom resident in God's domain, the Kingdom of God. You can never truly lose when you commit your life to advancing the Kingdom.

I have learned as a pastor, when I focus on building the Kingdom, my church grows automatically. Jesus builds His church, as He promised. He tells believers to seek the Kingdom, its advancement, victory, and success in every sphere of life— and the God of the Kingdom will add everything you need to experience life more abundantly.

KINGDOM PRAYER

As we continue our study of Kingdom principles in the next chapter, I invite you to pray with me:

> Dear Lord Jesus, thank you for coming to earth to restore the Kingdom of God. I ask you to help me to embrace your parables and to receive greater revelation of your Kingdom purposes through understanding your teachings. Help me to focus on seeking first your Kingdom. Let me receive your promise that "all these things will be added" to me. I want to become a God-carrier, filled with your love and spreading your glory on the earth. Thank you for your truth that sets me free to fulfill my destiny. In Your name, amen.

KINGDOM PRINCIPLES
FROM CHAPTER 3

1. Jesus' parables illustrate the nature of the Kingdom, revealing the King's generosity and benevolent kindness to those who seek the Kingdom.
2. The laws and principles of the Kingdom that Jesus taught did not remotely resemble the religious lifestyle of the day.
3. In His parables, Jesus compared and contrasted the realities of the Kingdom of God with the common pursuits of mankind in every sphere of life.
4. Through these vivid dramas of life, Jesus continually revealed the nature of His Father's Kingdom, showing the love of the Father, His humility, generosity, kindness and mercy.
5. As a believer, Jesus taught that the Kingdom of heaven is first of all within you (Luke 17:21), working like leaven to transform your nature so that it reflects the character of God.
6. The man-made hierarchy, placing greater value on the service of clergy than on other spheres of service is not Biblical.
7. As a born again believer, you are destined to reflect God's glory and subdue the earth, bringing it back to His rule.
8. Christ is looking for Christians who are addicted to and

obsessed by their desire for the supremacy and reign of the King in his domain, the Kingdom of God.

9. When God finds a person who will abandon themselves fearlessly, with all their resources, intelligence, and strength, to promote the Kingdom of God, He will respond by throwing all the weight and authority of His Kingdom behind them to extend His Kingdom through them.

10. Life pursuits become platforms—"pulpits"—to be able to declare Kingdom principles and demonstrate the Kingdom lifestyle of a man or woman restored to the Kingdom of God and restoring the Kingdom of God on the earth.

Chapter 4

PRINCIPLES OF THE KINGDOM

Thou shalt love the Lord thy God with all thy heart, and with all thy soul, and with all thy mind. This is the first and great commandment. And the second is like unto it, Thou shalt love thy neighbour as thyself.

—MATTHEW 37–39

The Kingdom of God is a spiritual reality, filled with divine power to transform individual lives, communities, and nations. As we begin to understand the purpose for God's Kingdom on the earth, from the beginning of time, we can begin to appreciate the privilege we have as born again believers to extend the Kingdom of God in our world. As we realize the priority of the Kingdom of God—the passion of His heart—we can only be moved to worship Him. The love of the Father for each of us and the unfathomable treasures of His Kingdom, especially as revealed in Jesus' parables, should cause us to surrender our lives unreservedly to fulfill His will on the earth.

Still, many Christians do not reflect a Kingdom lifestyle that reveals the passion of God's heart for the world. As I observed earlier, entire churches are built to enshrine the personality and fulfill the agenda of the pastor, without giving consideration to the real needs of the community. Sadly, many religious people do not understand the eternal purposes of God regarding His Kingdom coming to earth. That is because these divine truths cannot be understood by the natural intellect; the Spirit of God must reveal them to our redeemed spirit. The scriptures state this fact clearly:

> For what man knoweth the things of a man, save the spirit of man, which is in him? Even so the things of God knoweth no man, but the Spirit of God. Now we have received, not the spirit of the world, but the Spirit which is of God; that we might know the things that are freely given to us of God...But the natural man receiveth not the things of the Spirit of God: for they are foolishness unto him: neither can he know them, because they are spiritually discerned.
> **—1 CORINTHIANS 2:11–12, 14**

Many Christians do not reflect a Kingdom lifestyle

As we consider the foundational principles of the Kingdom of God, we need to realize that the Spirit of God must reveal these underlying, divine truths to us. Intellectual assent will never substitute for the passion of a heart that yearns to know God and to help others to know Him. When we receive the Spirit of God into our lives, we can begin to know "the things that are freely given to us of God". Out of the intimacy of that personal relationship with God will burst forth our passionate desire to be a part of extending His principles for living on the earth.

The Holy Spirit will teach us how to share the treasures of the Kingdom in our sphere of life. We will learn how to present principles of righteousness to others that brings healing and wholeness, without alienating people because of our religious dogma, traditions and empty creeds. Religious practices and doctrinal issues cannot take precedence over presenting Kingdom principles to lost people. When that happens, we become like the Pharisees whom Jesus accused of shutting up the Kingdom of heaven so that people could not get in (Matt. 23:13). Unfortunately, much of the church's approach today has had the effect of shutting up the Kingdom to needy souls.

When Jesus taught the principles of the Kingdom of God, He challenged people to embrace them in order to receive eternal life. He promised them life more abundantly (Jn. 10:10), filled with fruitfulness, peace, joy, and love. It is amazing that anyone could have turned down such an opportunity for "heaven on earth" in relationship with the King of Kings. Unfortunately today we often present our religious practices and dogmas to people instead of the Kingdom and its values. Hence, many do not want to have anything to do with the church.

UNDERSTANDING KINGDOM PRINCIPLES

Earlier I wrote that you are hard-wired for the Kingdom of God. I explained that the principles of the Kingdom are inherent to all of life and cannot be violated without suffering consequences. From the natural laws like gravity to the spiritual laws of love and forgiveness, Kingdom principles still rule the universe. They cannot be altered or broken; they do not change. Violating them, either in ignorance or willfully, results in self-

119

destruction.

A principle is defined simply by Webster's Dictionary as "a comprehensive and fundamental law; a rule or code of conduct". It is important that you are able to clearly define and present Kingdom principles to others, especially to those who have no apparent interest in "religion." Kingdom principles have as little to do with religion today as they did in Jesus' day. Today, even in the face of governmental leaders who call for "separation of Church and State", believers can learn to practice and to present to others as well, the fundamental laws of the Kingdom of God.

A principle is a coprehensive and fundmental law; a rule or code of conduct.

A NEW COMMANDMENT

When Jesus declared "A new commandment I give unto you, that ye love one another; as I have loved you, that ye also love one another", He was articulating the most fundamental principle of the Kingdom of God. In that commandment, He defined the nature of His Kingdom, based in the essence of who God is: "God is love" (1 Jn 4:8). And He was stating the priority of the Kingdom regarding our relationship to others: "that ye also love one another". This comprehensive law of love is to be reflected in every attitude, word, and action of our lives as believers. That divine love must characterize the message of the gospel wherever it is preached, in the marketplace as well as in pulpits.

Jesus presented the realities of the Kingdom of God without the religious dogma, creeds, or man-made practices of the Jewish religion that had become so oppressive to its adherents. His answer to all of life's complexities was simply to "Seek ye first the Kingdom of God and his righteousness" (Matt. 6:33). And He condemned the religious leaders of the day for their wrong motivation and oppression of the people:

> The scribes and the Pharisees sit in Moses' seat: All therefore whatsoever they bid you observe, that observe and do; but do not ye after their works: for they say, and do not. For they bind heavy burdens and grievous to be borne, and lay them on men's shoulders; but they themselves will not move them with one of their fingers. But all their works they do for to be seen of men...
>
> **—MATTHEW 23:2–5**

Jesus told the people to observe the teachings of the religious leaders, as they were faithful to communicate the Law of Moses. But He warned them not to imitate the motivation or works of these proud, uncaring men who loved to lord it over the people, considering themselves to be superior, and requiring heavy "religious" burdens of the people. Their actions could be compared to the church dogma of our day that interprets the scriptures legalistically and requires certain external codes of conduct, separating believers into denominations to protect those theological positions. Too many religious leaders have promoted religion without making the law of Love the foundational principle and priority of their lives.

FOUNDATIONAL PRINCIPLES

Jesus presented the comprehensive truth of the Kingdom of God in two parallel aspects:

1. The gospel of salvation, which He was to accomplish

through His death at Calvary and His resurrection. The purpose of salvation is to transfer us from the kingdom of darkness to His Kingdom, the Kingdom of light

2. The gospel of the Kingdom. This is the Kingdom, the inheritance Jesus bought for us where we have our citizenship and the responsibility to extend this Kingdom, restoring the earth through the values and principles of the Kingdom.

Unfortunately, most preaching today centers around the first aspect: the gospel of salvation. There is little understanding of the second aspect of Jesus' teaching regarding what we are saved to. This is described as the gospel of the Kingdom. I do not mean to imply that there are two gospels; there are not. That was never the intent of Jesus' message. However, because much of Christendom is preaching only half of the gospel, which is how we are transferred, neglecting the second part, which is where we are saved to. The result is that those of us who are preaching the whole gospel of the Kingdom may seem to be presenting a "second gospel". That is a result of the failure of the modern church to grasp the significance of Jesus' message of salvation and of the Kingdom.

This lack of understanding the whole gospel is not a new problem. The writer to the Hebrews introduced us to this problem of focusing on a "half gospel". He admonished believers to grow up:

Therefore leaving the principles of the doctrine of Christ, let us go on unto perfection; not laying again the foundation of repentance from dead works, and of faith toward God, of the doctrine of baptisms, and of laying on of hands, and of resurrection of the dead, and of eternal judgment. And this will we do, if God permit..

—HEBREWS 6:1–3

According to this passage, the writer to the Hebrews calls certain teachings foundational principles of Christ regarding eternal salvation. And he admonishes believers to go on to perfection, not just focusing on these foundational teachings of the Kingdom of God. There are six principles or divine laws, referenced in this passage, which are basic teachings of Christianity:

1. Repentance.
2. Faith
3. Baptisms
4. Laying on of hands
5. Resurrection of the dead
6. Eternal judgment

The scripture refers to these principles as foundational (Heb. 6:1). They pertain to what I call the gospel of salvation or the first aspect of the Kingdom of God that Jesus preached regarding how we are transferred. Unfortunately, these are the only principles that many churches today are teaching and preaching.

There are many churches that teach only repentance unto salvation: "You must be born again." Then after people are born again, these pastors focus on finding ways to keep people in church, making them good church members and occupying them with the activities of the church. Even their evangelistic efforts are simply to get more people to receive the gospel of salvation and become church members. Sound familiar? This is the entire focus of many churches today. They are oblivious to the "second half" of the gospel, which tells us what to do in the Kingdom, and that Jesus articulated in His prayer: "Thy Kingdom come. Thy will be done on earth, as it is in heaven" (Matt. 6:10).

UNDERSTANDING THE "GOSPEL"

When Jesus spoke of the end of the world, He declared that it would not come until the gospel of the Kingdom had been preached in all the world:

> And this gospel of the kingdom shall be preached in all the world for a witness unto all nations; and then shall the end come.
>
> **—MATTHEW 24:14**

The word "gospel" in the Greek language simply means "a good message" (Strong's 2098: euaggelion). The gospel is the good news about something. I could bring you the good news that my wife is going to have a baby. That is good news; it is gospel. But Jesus qualified the use of the word gospel with a specific assignment to preach the gospel of the Kingdom of God:

> Let the dead bury their dead: but go thou and preach the kingdom of God.
>
> **—LUKE 9:60**

After the foundational truths of salvation are believed and received, according to the scriptures, we are to move forward and go on to perfection. Maturing in our faith involves becoming ambassadors for Christ to bring the reality of His Kingdom to earth and to fulfill the will of God in earth—as it is in heaven. Extending these principles of the Kingdom on the earth is the destiny of every believer

Because we have not understood the relationship between establishing a local church and extending Kingdom principles throughout the whole earth, we have settled for something less than the gospel of the Kingdom. It leaves people in a state of salvation without understanding the work they have to do. The church is not the Kingdom, which we will discuss more in the next chapter. The church is the body of Christ on the earth whose mandate is to promote the Kingdom and extend Kingdom principles in every sphere of life.

Few leaders are preaching this message of the Kingdom. They simply preach the message of salvation. This misunderstanding of the gospel diminishes the priority and power of the Kingdom. Many Christians tell me after I teach the gospel of the Kingdom that they have never heard anything about the Kingdom, though they have attended church all their lives. They have been taught about repentance, faith, baptisms, and other foundational teachings. But they have not heard of the aspect of the gospel that involves the restoration of the values, lifestyle, and principles of the Kingdom to their family, their community, and beyond. Establishing love, integrity, justice, and righteousness in every sphere of life where we have influence is the way believers fulfill the petition: "Thy kingdom come. Thy will be done on earth as it is in heaven" (Matt. 6:10).

REDEMPTION OF THE WORLD

When Adam and Eve sinned, God did not curse the man; He cursed the earth, so that it is bearing the consequences of the sin of the man. Because of that curse, life is difficult for everyone. Thorns and thistles sprang forth from the ground instead of the exquisiteness of the vegetation in the Garden of Eden. God told Adam:

Cursed is the ground for your sake; In toil you shall eat
of it all the days of your life. Both thorns and thistles
it shall bring forth for you, and you shall eat the herb
of the field. In the sweat of your face you shall eat
bread...

—GENESIS 3:17–19

Jesus gave his life to redeem mankind from the effects of
sin. While that victory does not immediately restore the earth
the pristine state of the garden of Eden, it does restore the
responsibility of believers for stewardship for the earth. And
it gives us resonsibility to work to redeem society from the ills
stemming from irresponsibility and other faces of sin.

God did not curse man; He cursed the earth.

The Holy Spirit deals with lost souls, desiring to save them
and nurture their faith to maturity in the image of Christ, thus
fulfilling the foundational principles of the Kingdom taught by
the church. The church is also to be led by the Holy Spirit to
empower and equip believers to bring the values of the Kingdom
to the sphere of life in which they have influence. As they mature
in the love of God, they become God-carriers, Ambassadors for
Christ, reconciling people to God and together with the passion
and the power changing even the environment and atmosphere
of society. This is how we serve others in love.

Transformation of society, subduing the kingdom of darkness
to the dominion of the Kingdom of light is the assignment—the
destiny and responsibility—of the church. We are called to extend
the love of God to all and the values of the Kingdom into our
troubled society filled with fatherless children, confused teens,
unwed mothers, broken marriages, faulty educational systems,

corrupt business enterprises, and greedy governmental policies. This is what Jesus meant by His command to "Let your light so shine before men, that they may see your good works, and glorify your Father which is in heaven" (Matt. 5:16).

Heather Veitch is a loveable x-stripper turned evangelist. She started a ministry to help women in the sex industries. Her mission of love persuaded a young Christian pastor and a few women from her church to join her. Heather calls her group JC's Girls and started taking the team to strip clubs and porn conventions for outreach to lap dancers, hookers and porn queens.

Ironically, the sex industry welcomes JC's Girls but powerful forces in the Christian church refuse to tolerate Heather's "immoral ministry." She receives hate mail and death threats accusing her of being a fame seeking "Fake" who is softening the gospel. But she refuses to back down from her mission, producing a documentary film called The Pussycat Preacher, which won an "Audience Favorite" award at the 2008 Cinequest Film Festival. Out of 285 films in competition for this award, Pussycat Preacher won by a margin of 3 to 1. It is a story that is sometimes sad and other times funny, but all true. It cuts to the core of issues of faith, love, and tolerance.

Heather is allowing the redeeming love of God that rescued her to give her a platform among the "untouchables" of her social sphere, for which the some in the church seemingly had no answer and less regard.

Porn industry is Heather's ministry. She didn't shy away from it because she believes that the God in her is greater than the evil in the industry, her light is stronger than the darkness there. Some of these people would not have had another chance of hearing the gospel since they won't go to church.

REDEEMING THE SOCIAL SPHERE THROUGH NGO'S AND NPO'S

The assignment of every believer in presenting the gospel—the good news of the Kingdom—is to become responsible for his or her "promised land". That is, they are to function effectively in their place of destiny where they wield the power of Kingdom principles to transform their environment through their godly lifestyle. In this way believers can impact people in every dimension of society: education, government, music, business, and every sphere of society with the love, peace, joy and righteousness of God. The Kingdom of God must not be limited to the four walls of the church.

As a pastor in Europe, I have discovered that it has become more and more difficult to witness and evangelize openly in the society. This is because open testimony and witness is considered an "anti-social" behavior, especially in Europe. In a situation such as this, where you are not allowed to voice your faith openly, we in the Embassy of God have discovered that one of the most effective ways of bringing the gospel to even the hardest social citadels is through social organizations, known in some countries as Non –Government Organizations (NGO's) or Non-Profit Organizations (NPO's).

As a result, thanks to this strategy, our church now has NPOs for everything! Members of The Embassy of God have established over 3, 000 functioning organizations, of which 600 are registered with the government. They vary from social organizations for drug addicts, alcoholics, abused women, single mothers, needy families, former prostitutes, teachers, youth, teenagers, to just anything that anybody has a burden for.

This is so important because church organization, seen as a religious institutions, are most often not allowed to openly bring the gospel to places such as schools, prisons, etc.. But through social organizations that don't have a religious face, we have been able to have an impact on lives that goes beyond what any pastor could have done from the pulpit. This is what it means to be the church outside of the four walls of our church organizations.

Serving Prisoners

One of the social organizations is for prisoners lead by Yuriy who was captured and imprisoned for his illegal activities. He was known as the "godfather" of the Kyivskiy mafia family. As he served time in prison, he came to know Christ through the Embassy of God's prison programs. As he pursued his relationship with Christ, he became a prison pastor. Now he has been released from prison and continues to train pastors to minister in prisons. He has hundreds of pastors who are now ministering in prisons in Ukraine.

These one-time social outcasts are redeeming men and women from the dark world of crime by presenting the light of the gospel, the principles of the Kingdom of God. The love of God that reached into the once-darkened heart and mind of Yuriy is now being shed abroad to thousands of lost souls in the Ukrainian prison system. Yuriy was not content to receive the peace of God for his own soul; his passion is to alleviate the suffering of his "fellow prisoners." He has become a mature believer, equipped to bring the Kingdom of God to earth and restore the will of God to many who sat in darkness. Today there are over 10,000 beleivers in prisons through the ministry of Yuriy, in over a hundred prisons.

When prisoners receive Christ and begin to share His love instead of their hatred, Satan loses ground. Society is much safer and becomes a healthier environment because of the salvation of these troubled men and women. This is a powerful example of restoring the Kingdom of God to the earth and transforming society.

To help you consider where your "promised land" might be found, I have listed here a few of the more than 600 social organizations we have registered with the government, with a brief description of their mission:

Victory Is In Your Hands

Pastor Roman Trohin and his "daughter church" of the Embassy of God founded the rehabilitation center, 'Victory Is In Your Hands'. For more than 5 years, Pastor Trohin and his team have been making the most of their civil position and influencing the society life of their city, working to change the lives of addicts and their families. Through this rehabilitation center, thousands of peope have asked for help and received it. During the summer, they organize a rehabilitation tent camp. The forestry organization, Staro-Petrovskoe, has heped their cause by giving them a section of forest on the bank of Kyiv reservoir. Other businesses have donated money for tents and other equipment necessary for campground living.

In just two summers, over 100 addicts participating in the tent camp were rehabilitated and able to return to their families. Members of the center have organized a fast-food restaurant called "Smachno" (Tasty), using the profits to support the rehabilitation program. Leaders of "Victory is in Your Hands" are also working with children to teach them how to live a healthy life of joy and peace, according to Christian ethics and Kingdom principles. The center takes care of children with HIV and counsels with their parents. This organization also organizes discos for young people along with other wholesome activities. And they are helping the poor and restoring the land through such projects as planting seedlings at boarding schools. They also carry out preventive inspections for narcotics, alcoholism, dangerous activities and prostitution. Every year more than 8,000 people and students are touched through this organization, which has visited 20 schools, 4 colleges and the Academy of Police of Ukraine. The rehabilitation center also offers spiritual and psychological help to patients of tuberculosis dispensaries.

Svoboda (Freedom)

Valery used to be a criminal and a drug-addict. Today he is a pastor and a missionary in Vepryk village. He sees the great potential in the outcasts of society when redeemed by the power of God. More than 600 people went through this rehabilitation center within the first 2 years of its operation. Leaders conduct social work in 56 schools and in 34 places around the Kyiv and the Zhytomir regions, Borodynka area and Byelorussia. So remarkable are the success stories of former addicts that the administrators of Nesolon village in Novograd-Volynsky area have granted the rehabilitation center 4 hectares (about 10 acres) of land!

Leaders of Svoboda have compiled the following statistics from different towns in of Ukraine, and Russia, showing how many people have been helped from far and near:
- 300 drug-addicts
- 210 alcoholics
- 50 people in depression
- 30 schizophrenics
- 23 gamblers

Valery not only helps them to become free from addictions, but also prepares them to be leaders and ministers. Some of them have become directors of similar rehabilitation centers. A prayer house, which is being built by former addicts a couple of meters from the rehab center, is a tribute to the freedom God has given them. Once slaves of sin and saved today, they have been set free from addictions and are willing to praise God through their works. Work therapy helps those who have never worked to become working people. Through work to obedience, through obedience to humility, through humility to reflect the glory of God! The local newspapers are writing articles today about these outcasts that no one once wanted to remember.

Today they have established 500 rehabilitation centers in Ukraine and raised up a wonderful team that is prepared to go anywhere in the world. As a result, the devil has lost many "servants" who perpetrated crime and misery on society.

To understand the great work of God in Valery's life, it might help you to know that he actually came to the church the first time to kill me. Armed with two pistols he was breathing fire because I had led his younger brother to Christ. This was regarded as a great insult to the Georgian Republic Mafia family. The only answer for that was to eliminate the source of threat to the family dynasty. As he was about to enter our church building, he suddenly collapsed with a heart attack. In the hospital he had an encounter with Jesus, and the rest, as they say is history...

Posol +

"Posol+" is a social organization that carries out various social missions including:

- Prevention teachings in schools – more than 4 thousand pupils have heard the truth about the negative influence of drugs, alcohol, smoking and abortions.
- Consultation and rehabilitation – in afternoon and evening classes in outpatient settings for alcohol and drug addicts and their families, more than 700 addicted people received consultations, about 200 people have gone through

rehabilitation, and 50 of them have become free today.

- Rehabilitation of prisoners – working with prison officials, more than 1,100 convicts and people under investigation have gone through trainings and individual consultations.
- Help for the homeless - about 500 homeless people have received food, medical and psychological help. In November, 2007 a permanent establishment for homeless people was put into operation.

Posol+ actively cooperates with local government bodies such as City council and social services and Illegal Drug Circulation Control Institution. They have staged peaceful demonstrations outside of pharmacies and other places that sold illegal painkillers containing opium. As a result the illegal sale of Tramadol was stopped. On another occasion, a demonstration of "Women Against Drugs" was conducted, with a wailing wall erected in the center square of Lviv filled with pictures of deceased drug-addicts and alcoholics, along with deformed children born to drug-addicted people.

These activities have gained much publicity, with 33 articles about the work of the organization being published in notable periodicals and 12 television programs have broadcast their efforts on leading channels in the city.

David musical school

Most of today's society is involved in some form of musical expression, much of which today is destructive to the human psyche. In 1999, Natalia founded the International Charitable Fund of Development of Musical Art and Spiritual Cultur David musical school in Kiev. In 2000 the musical educational center, David musical school, was opened with the goal to train singers and musicians professionally and spiritually to serve in churches as well as social spheres of art and culture.

Natalia is not simply trying to utilize her vocation, but to influence thousands of other peoples' artistic careers. They work with representatives of major artistic spheres such as music, literature, art, cinematography, theatre, circus and others. The goal of the foundation is to extend God's Kingdom in the sphere of art and culture. The best teachers from Ukrainian musical institutes of higher education work at this center. Their goal is to open branches of the center in more than 100 countries of the world.

Prophylaxis' Ministry (Preventive Health Services)

Even though religion and schools are separate in Ukraine, NGOs such as Prophylaxis' ministry are able to bring the Kingdom of God effectively to youth through educational facilities. Volunteers of the Prophylaxis' ministry go to the secondary schools with lectures about the destructiveness of smoking, alcoholism and drugs, as well as abortion and crimes among youth. Today this ministry has over 200 youth employed to work in the county's social system. At least 25,000 youth hear their lectures weekly.

They work with Headmasters and Administrators of Social and Educational facilities, presenting their curricula to them. Many of these city leaders give testimony to the effectiveness of the discussions and youth activities that are being offered. These are having a significant impact on the youth of their city. Helping youth to preserve and cultivate a healthy lifestyle, based on principles of the Kingdom is a tremendous help to the future of society, as educators understand.

My prayer is that by relating to you a few of the specific ways that believers are making a difference in their communities, bringing people into the Kingdom and together extending the

Kingdom of God in their promised land in various spheres of society, you will be inspired and helped to discover where you can make a difference as well.

Destined for Transformation

As a believer, you cannot function effectively without becoming a responsible member of the body of Christ on the earth—the church. Having said that, your primary responsibility is not to grow your church; your primary responsibility is to extend the Kingdom, which we will explore in more detail in the next chapter.

When you are born again and come to the church, you are responsible to dedicate yourself to receive the foundational principles taught by member of the church. Then, you must become responsible bring others into the Kingdom and to spread the principles and lifestyle of the Kingdom of God to the sphere of influence you have been given. For example, to fulfill your destiny means to saturate the vocation to which you have been called with the principles of the Kingdom. Your influence on your colleagues, as well as on your family and friends, with the lifestyle of the Kingdom of God will bring more people into the Kingdom and bring about the transformation to your community.

As a mature believer, your calling is not just to sing in the church choir, become an usher, or participate in another church-oriented service. If you have an anointing or giftings for musical expression, of course you should make them available in your church gatherings. As you gather, serve in any way that you can. But that is not to be your primary or only "ministry."

Too many Christians have adopted the erroneous "religious philosophy" that they are called to minister to the church, while others are called to be missionaries the world. That is not Biblically correct. The reason the Kingdom of God is in your heart is so that you can spread the glory of God throughout the earth where you have been given influence. That is the meaning of the Great Commission: "Go ye into all the world, and preach the gospel to every creature" (Mk. 16:15). That command is not given to missionaries or just specific, specially called individuals; it is a command for all believers. Serving each other when we gather does not somehow exempt us from the resonsibility to go into all the world. We are all are obliged to carry the great commission out as followers of Christ.

As a mature believer you are not called just to serve those within the   church.

As a mature believer, you are supposed to be committed to the increase of the Kingdom in the world, to the victory of the Kingdom of God over the kingdom of darkness. That is not the same as increasing your visibility or position or influence in the gatherings of the local church. The glory of God is extended through believers throughout the earth so that, as the prophet declared, "...the earth shall be filled with the knowledge of the glory of the LORD, as the waters cover the sea" (Hab. 3:14).

For example in the Embassy of God we established an institute called "The Center for the Restoration of Personality and Societal Transformation". We encourage every member of the church who is a mature Christian and feels the burden to do something more significant in society to study at this center.

There they are taught how to minister to the needs of people and restore their personalities, to see them transformed by the power of God and become world changers who will go and transform the society. This curriculum has helped so many people who graduated from the center to find their calling, gifting, talents, and thereby make a positive contribution to the local society. They have since graduated over 12,000 students.

Melnik Victoria, a student of the Word, has dedicated her entire life to this task. Her influence is felt broadly as a citizen of Ukraine who is president of this large social organization, in the science sphere as a professor in the State Academy, and in educational circles as author of many scientific articles, methodology manuals, and texts for higher education.

The Center for Personality and Social transformation gives unique opportunity to explore the basis of human nature and introduce Kingdom values and principles to forge a healthy society. The Center has become a very powerful educational institution and a bridge between broken society and the church.

As the president of this Center, Victoria is using her God-given ability and wisdom to develop strong powerful leaders. She has gathered a talented team of scientists, lawyers, doctors, political leaders, and sportsmen, who lead more than 50 affiliates in 9 countries. They are transforming lives in various spheres of influence.

"Ingrown" Focus

For too many pastors, the focus of their ministry becomes ingrown; they are completely absorbed in church activities. They get people saved and then figure out what they can do to establish them in attendance and giving to their church. They try to give them something to do in the church that will make them feel important and needed. They teach them not to go back to the world because the world is bad. While there is truth in all of these approaches, the end result is for the pastor to build his church and help people make it to heaven as their central focus instead of extending the Kingdom throughout the earth.

This can result in church leaders exploiting members to build a big church, in order to bring more people into their church gatherings. They create unceasing activity, entertainment, and even "good deeds" to make people feel useful. These church-centered tactics result in a "closed" church, in-fighting, jostling for position, and sometimes church splits.

Willow Creek Community Church, located in Northwest-suburban Chicago, Illinois, was founded by Bill Hybels over 30 years ago. It is a non-denominational church with weekly attendance of about 23,500, according to Hartford Seminary's database of megachurches. It is considered one of the top three most influential churches in America. Willow Creek was designed specifically for "seekers" or what they call "people far from God." Known as the "seeker-friendly" movement, the Willow Creek Association has been influential for thousands of churches who purchased their resources and adopted their approach because of its "apparent success."

While it is to be commended for its passion to see unchurched people become followers of Jesus, recently its founder, Bill Hybels, apologized publicly for "making a mistake" in their approach to winning the lost. According to research involving their church attendees, the multitude of activities they have continually provided, the millions of dollars they spent on their program-driven church to inspire participation, has not resulted in mature believers who love God and seek Him.

After spending thirty years creating and promoting a multi-million dollar organization driven by programs and measuring participation, and convincing other church leaders to do the same, Hybels confesses:

We made a mistake. What we should have done when people crossed the line of faith and become Christians, we should have started telling people and teaching people that they have to take responsibility to become 'self feeders.' We should have...taught people how to read their Bible...how to do the spiritual practices much more aggressively on their own... Our dream is that we fundamentally change the way we do church. That we take out a clean sheet of paper and we rethink all of our old assumptions. Replace it with new insights... Our dream is really to discover what God is doing and how he's asking us to transform this planet.

While this humble confession may bring a needed adjustment to the "seeker friendly" movement, it has not addressed the core issue for fulfilling the Biblical mandate of the church. As we have discussed, the role of leadership in the church, according to the scriptures, is to equip the saints for the work of the ministry. It is to teach believers to become God-carriers to extend the Kingdom throughout the earth.

In other words, not only does participating in elaborate church programs that focus on building the church not bring people to true holiness and a mature fear of God, it does not address the true, scriptural mandate of every believer. As leaders we have to equip believers to become God-carriers, to take the life of God to the world. Believers must understand their destiny to bring others into the Kingdom and to together transform their sphere of life through the principles of the Kingdom by becoming salt and light to the world.

Forgotten in this priority of seeker-sensitive church-building are the purposes of God that his will would be done in earth as it is in heaven, reclaiming the earth for the Kingdom of God. This is to equip members to reclaim the territory—to take it from Satan, establishing Kingdom principles, lifestyle, atmosphere and environment, in every institution and expression of life. This is to restore every sphere of life to a God-centered philosophy and transform the world of finance, politics, the arts, entertainment, education, medicine, social services into God-centered entities.

Focusing totally on the gospel of salvation requires keeping members from becoming bored as they go about the endless task of focusing on church activities. Leaders teach members to submit to complete obedience to the church philosophy and its priorities. Sometimes they warn against rebellion, which might include missing a church function to serve a needy person in the community. Leaders who teach only the foundational principles of salvation keep members coming to all their meetings, listening to the teaching, trying to keep them interested and involved. After a lifetime of service, they are often still listening, and focusing on their church's programs surrendering their in service to their church.

Instead of teaching people to seek first the Kingdom, which activates the promise that "all these things will be added", pastors try to keep members focused on the well-being of the gathering of local church. They teach that if they give generously to the church, their needs will be met. Some teach just keep giving to the church and you can have everything you want—the prosperity doctrine. So the members begin to pursue their desire for things: houses, cars, shoes, blackberries, plasma TVs. They think that because they are giving to the church, God is prospering them to seek after things.

Jesus prohibited us from seeking things, teaching that the gentiles, those who did not care about God, seek for things. He instructed us to seek first the Kingdom, to make the extending of His glory throughout the earth as our priority, our life pursuit, and our passion. Then, everything we need will be added as His provision for becoming a restorer of the Kingdom and the will of God on the earth. That is a different motivation from what is taught in many churches today.

This partial "gospel of salvation" which focuses only on growing the gatherings of believers has to a large extent put man back on the throne, focusing on his own life, his selfish interests and his own personal kingdom. Many churches teach believers that God wants to save you, then he wants to make you holy, then he wants to bless you—everything is about you. This becomes a man-centered message, which teaches people to come to church to get their needs met, to have a spiritual experience, to feel good about themselves. So God becomes a stepping stone to get what they want—to make their lives better. As a result, being a Christian is not about serving God; it is about God serving them. So God is not God; you are god and demanding that God serve you.

In America, the widely popular "seeker-sensitive" approach to bringing unsaved people to church focuses on felt needs of the people, including questions facing life such as job, family, relationships. Sermons are designed to help a person to live more fully and successfully in a hectic society. The service is designed to be entertaining, non-threatening, and focusing on needs of the people. People come to church to get God to meet their personal needs, like some "genie in a bottle."

D. Martyn Lloyd-Jones (1899-1981), pastor of Westminster Chapel in London, wrote, "Any teaching…that starts with us and our needs, rather than the glory of God, is unscriptural, and seriously unscriptural. That subjective approach… is what has led many astray for so many years". Being 'seeker-sensitive' and leaving out the message of Jesus as Lord is an incomplete and anemic gospel.

A man-centered message teaches people to come to church to get their needs met, to have a spiritual experience, to feel good about themselves.

THE PRINCIPLE OF LORDSHIP

Those who preach the whole gospel understand that when we receive Christ we also make Him Lord of our lives. This principle of the Kingdom involves the cost of discipleship, which Jesus taught clearly:

> Then said Jesus unto his disciples, if any man will come after me, let him deny himself, and take up his cross, and follow me. For whosoever will save his life shall lose it: and whosoever will lose his life for my sake shall find it.
>
> **—MATTHEW 16:24**

> Verily, verily, I say unto you, except a corn of wheat fall into the ground and die, it abideth alone: but if it die, it bringeth forth much fruit. He that loveth his life shall lose it; and he that hateth his life in this world shall keep it unto life eternal.
>
> **—JOHN 12:24–25**

The whole gospel involves the principle of making Christ Lord of your life, dethroning self, putting Christ on the throne, taking up your cross, and following Him. Jesus said, "If any man serve me, let him follow me; and where I am, there shall also my servant be: if any man serve me, him will my Father honour" (John 12:26).

When we receive Christ we also make Him Lord of our life.

Churches that are filled with Christians who are honoring themselves are not worshiping God; they are worshiping themselves. That is called idolatry. Many churches are filled with idol worshipers who think they are going to heaven. Which heaven, the one you created? We cannot violate the principle of Lordship, discipleship, or any other Kingdom principle without suffering the consequences of deception and defeat. If we are not pursuing God and His purposes, becoming addicted to His Kingdom priority, we are merely serving God to be blessed by Him and "using" Him to meet our needs.

The Kingdom reality is that God is the sovereign Lord; I am His slave, a tool in His hands. He is Love, and I am created for Him and to extend the benefits of the Kingdom as an act of love. I can know no greater blessing than to be a servant in His benevolent Kingdom.

John the Revelator had a glimpse into heaven and saw the twenty-four elders falling down before the throne of God, casting their crowns before Him and saying:

> Thou are worthy, O Lord, to receive glory and honour and power: for thou hast created all things, and for thy pleasure they are and were created.
> **—REVELATION 4:11**

And the apostle Paul revealed the pre-eminence of Christ in his prayer for the Colossian church:

> ...Giving thanks unto the Father, which hath made us meet to be partakers of the inheritance of the saints in light: Who hath delivered us from the power of darkness, and hath translated us into the kingdom of his dear Son: In whom we have redemption through his blood, even the forgiveness of sins: Who is the image of the invisible God, the firstborn of every creature:

143

> For by him were all things created, that are in heaven, and that are in earth, visible and invisible, whether they be thrones, or dominions, or principalities, or powers: all things were created by him, and for him: And he is before all things, and by him all things consist. And he is the head of the body, the church: who is the beginning, the firstborn from the dead; that in all things he might have the preeminence.
>
> **—COLOSSIANS 1:12–18**

Creator of all things, Savior of all mankind, the Head of the body, the church—Christ has pre-eminence over all. As redeemed sons and daughters of the King, our priority, our passion, our addiction, our life-pursuit is to be centered in extending the Kingdom of Love and Light throughout the whole earth. "Then, what about my needs?" you ask. When I submit my life to the Lordship of Christ, there is no problem with receiving what I need. When I seek the advancement of His Kingdom and the victory of his Kingdom, 'all these things will be added'—that is the promise of the King. And I have proved that reality in every area of my personal life.

The Kingdom reality is that God is the sovereign Lord; I am His slave

The foundational principles of repentance, faith, and baptisms are good; we need them. But many churches have distorted the purpose for them. We don't repent just to join a church. Repentance is for the purpose of gaining entrance to the Kingdom. Faith is absolutely necessary for every believer; the scriptures declare that without faith we cannot please God (Heb. 11:6). Yet, faith is not to be used primarily to get what you want from God; it is to make it possible for you to please God.

How do we please God? We please God when we do His will. What I cannot do in my own strength to extend His Kingdom rule, I am able to believe God to do through me, to make me His channel, to become an instrument to bring His will to pass on the earth, to do exploits that are not possible for man. You can use your faith to buy a new car; I will use my faith to win a nation to Him. The purpose of faith is to empower you to fulfill divine destiny, as Abraham did, who believed God and became a father of nations.

The foundational principle of baptisms—baptism, baptism in the Holy Spirit—is vital to every believer. We need to understand all the basic foundations of the Kingdom, for empowering us to go on to perfection. We are sent into the world as Jesus was sent, to establish the Kingdom of God througout the earth. We are to become God carriers, Kingdom carriers into every sphere of life. According to the words of Jesus, until this gospel of the Kingdom is preached, He will not return to earth.

I am on a journey, I am a crusader determined to change the faulty concepts of "church as usual". I am challenging believers to embrace the gospel of the Kingdom that requires that they live for the King only, that they embrace the principle of His Lordship, which involves personal discipleship, and restoring people to the Kingdom and together restoring the domain of the earth to the King of Kings—Christ Jesus our Lord.

This Kingdom message is the priority, the heartbeat of God, and should become ours as well. We are to leave behind the basics, the fundamental principles and go on to maturity to be filled with the glory of God and be instruments to spread His glory over the whole earth. We are not to focus just on the benefits of the Kingdom, but to embrace the attributes, the character, the values, the principles, and the priority of restoring dominion of the earth to the King. This is the message of the Lordship of Jesus Christ.

It is all about God. Ultimately, it is not about the church. It is not about Christians. It is about God wanting to have a copy of heaven on the earth. God created the planet earth and mankind in His own image—to be just like Him. As God is managing the whole universe, He created mankind to manage the earth for Him, to have dominion over the earth as He does over the universe. That is why we are made in His image and likeness—to rule and be lord over the earth as He is Lord over the universe.

The scriptures call Jesus the last Adam (1 Cor. 15:45). One of the principles of the Creator is that small things contain the inherent ability to grow into larger ones. What started with one person is now 6 billion people in the world. So the Kingdom of God started in miniature in the Garden of Eden. What God had planned to do originally through Adam and Eve, He accomplished through His Son, Jesus.

He came to restore the original purpose of God, which is to bring the Kingdom from heaven to the earth and make the earth a reflection of heaven. When Jesus came He wanted us to rejoice that He had brought it back—the original purpose of God was being fulfilled. He had brought the Kingdom of heaven to earth in the miniature, a temporal reflection of an eternal reality, just like it was originally created in Adam.

What God had planned to do originally through Adam and Eve, He accomplished through His Son, Jesus.

Because mankind fell from grace through disobedience to the laws of the Kingdom, the glory of God was lost from the earth. When that divine glory was removed from the earth, Adam and Eve saw their nakedness. They were no longer covered by the presence of God. But Jesus brought back that glory and gave it to all who would receive Him, giving them the power to become children of God. And He established the church to equip the saints to do the work of the ministry, to establish the glory of God throughout the earth as He did. Christ promised that we would do greater works than He did because He went to the Father and gave us the Holy Spirit (Jn. 14:12).

We need the church to help us mature, to grow into sonship and not be children anymore. The scriptures instruct us to grow in the knowledge of God (Eph. 4:13). We are to study to show ourselves approved, workmen that need not be ashamed. (2 Tim. 2:15). We need to know the principles and truth of the Kingdom of God so that we can become immersed in doing the will of God. Then, we are to let our light shine in the darkness of this world so that many others can be redeemed.

As I wrote in my book, Churchshift, it is the principles of the Kingdom that bring people to Christ, without alienating them through religious dogma:

In five years, two million people have come to Christ at the altar of our church. We thank God that we are being used to win the lost, but the truly amazing thing is that this has not taken place through evangelism, crusades, or traditional methods of sharing the gospel. Rather, people have come to the church and come to Christ because of the example of many thousands of Christians putting Kingdom principles to work outside of the church. The heart of our discovery is that you don't need to promote religion or church for people to want to come to Christ. Rather, Kingdom principles will draw people. You don't even have to mention anything spiritual or religious—in fact, it's sometimes better not to. When you take God's principles into society, they simply work.

These principles of the Kingdom are not society or culture based; they are not limited to success in any specific type of political government or cultural mindset. The principles of the Kingdom are Biblical truth and they work for all of humanity when embraced by believers who learn to walk in them in obedience to the Great Commission.

The principles of the Kingdom work for all of humanity.

In order for the church to become the instrument of God for righteousness on the earth as it is ordained to become, leaders and believers alike must understand the Absolutism of the Kingdom and the Relativity of the Church. In the next chapter I will discuss the scriptural understanding of these two divine entities—The Kingdom and the church—and their relationship to each other in the eternal economy of God.

KINGDOM PRAYER

First, I invite you to pray with me again for divine revelation into the profound purpose of the Kingdom of God and your destiny as part of that Kingdom:

> Dear Jesus, please continue your work in my life to illuminate my mind and impact my heart with the passion of the your Father's heart. Let me be part of the answer to your petition: "Thy kingdom come. Thy will be done on earth as it is in heaven". Help me to embrace the principles of the Kingdom and influence those around me in such a way that they will desire to come to You; let me be a God-carrier to the sphere of life to which you have called me. Thank you, Lord. In your name I pray, amen.

KINGDOM PRINCIPLES
FROM CHAPTER 4

1. The Kingdom of God is a spiritual reality, filled with divine power to transform individual lives, communities, and nations.
2. The principles of the Kingdom must be revealed to us by the Holy Spirit.
3. Kingdom principles have as little to do with religion today as they did in Jesus' day.
4. Jesus presented the comprehensive truth of the Kingdom of God in two parallel aspects: The gospel of salvation and the gospel of the Kingdom.
5. Believers are admonished to go on to perfection, not focusing all their spiritual life on the foundational principles listed in Hebrews 6:1.
6. Jesus said the end would not come until the gospel of the Kingdom is preached in the whole world.
7. Transformation of society, subduing the kingdom of darkness to the dominion of the Kingdom of light is the assignment—the destiny—of the church.
8. To fulfill your destiny as a believer means to saturate the vocation to which you have been called with the principles of the Kingdom

9. The whole gospel involves the principle of making Christ Lord of your life, dethroning self, putting Christ on the throne, taking up your cross, and following Him.

10. As redeemed sons and daughters of the King, our priority, our passion, our addiction, our life-pursuit is to be centered in extending the Kingdom of Love and Light in the whole earth.

Chapter 5

PRE-EMINENCE OF THE KINGDOM

"...I will build my church; and the gates of hell shall not prevail against it. And I will give unto thee the keys of the kingdom of heaven..."

—MATTHEW 16:18–19

One of the greatest problems in the church is that many church leaders and believers alike think that the church and the Kingdom of God are synonymous terms. That misunderstanding is perhaps the greatest factor in the powerlessness, ingrown focus, and dead religiosity characterizing the church today. Many lack a clear understanding of the purpose of God to restore His Kingdom to the earth, and the church's role in fulfilling that mandate. For that reason, there is no clear definition of what a church should look like, especially in today's post-modern theological religious environment.

The basic premise of our discussion is that the church is not the ultimate end; it is a means to fulfill God's divine purpose. That purpose is for God's reign to be over all. This is because all creation was intended to be part of God's domain, his Kingdom. The culmination is for the will of God to be done on earth as it is done in heaven. That means for the principles of heaven to be reflected in the lifestyle of men on earth. It means for those principles that govern heaven to come and be used to rule over the earth. To bring part of heaven to be reflected on earth is the goal of creation; it is God's original intention.

The church is not the ultimate end; it is a means to fulfill God's divine purpose.

As I have mentioned, God created the earth for one purpose: to make the earth a copy or reflection of the Kingdom of God. The Garden of Eden was planned to be a a miniature reflection of the Kingdom of heaven. And the man was created in the image of God and assigned to rule, to have dominion, as the manager of the planet earth, just as God is the manager of the universe.

So when that plan failed because of Adam and Eve's fall, Jesus came to the earth to restore the original purpose of God. He came so that the Kingdom would be restored on earth, the "nakedness" of humanity would be covered, and the will of God would be done. Jesus brought the values, principles and lifestyle of the Kingdom to earth. He teaches us how to live in His Kingdom. His coming to earth restored the Kingdom of God to the earth. His perfect obedience to the Father's will, which ultimately took Him to the cross of Calvary to redeem us from our disobedience, succeeded in restoring the understanding of the Kingdom to us of God to earth.

Jesus gave the ultimate sacrifice on Calvary to conquer sin

that had ruled all of mankind through the disobedience of Adam and Eve. For those who would receive His resurrection reality, He gave them the Holy Spirit, filling them with the glory of God so that they might extend the presence of God, His dominion and rule, throughout the earth. He empowered believers in the early church to extend the character, principles, and lifestyle of the Kingdom wherever they went. Their entire lives would reflect the will of God who is in heaven, now residing in their spirit, to be released to fill the whole earth—the glory of God covering the earth as the waters that cover the sea.

In the domain of God, the Kingdom of God. is where we find the heartbeat of God, the dream of God, and His passion. It follows that those who are citizens of this domain who believe in Christ and call themselves Christians should be filled with that same dream, passion, and priority for life. They should be advancing the Kingdom where they are. Since God's will is for His values and the lifestyle of heaven to reign on the earth, those who name Him as their Father should reflect His will in who they are and all that they do. As a believer, the advancement, increase, and multiplication of the Kingdom of God should become the motivation, passion, and goal of your life pursuits.

THE CHURCH: THE GREATEST ORGANISM ON EARTH

The church is the greatest organism in the world. When empowered by the Spirit of God, the body of Christ is the most potent force on earth, endowed with divine authority to rule and reign according to the principles of the Kingdom of God. The church was formed to expand the Kingdom of God. It follows that the church is not the Kingdom of God, but citizens of the Kingdom of God.

The church is the hope of God for fulfilling His will and heartbeat that heaven's glory be extended once again throughout the whole earth. As the redeemed community of believers gather together to be equipped to do the work of the ministry, we are to restore the character and lifestyle and God's domain, the Kingdom of God on the earth as God originally planned.

The church is the greatest organism in the world

So how does the church fit into this heartbeat, this passion of God for the restoration of His Kingdom on earth? And why did Jesus say He would build His church? The church was birthed as citizens of the Kingdom and the instrument of God to advance His purpose for the Kingdom. Establishing the principles and lifestyle of the Kingdom of God, extending God's principles into every sphere of life, is the eternal purpose of the church, a key reason for its existence.

Jesus established the focus of the church on the Kingdom. He did not want us to misunderstand His mission and become self-serving instead of being focused on establishing the Kingdom of God. He taught only the Kingdom of God. He did not start His own religious movement or denomination during His ministry on earth. If He had, we would have built a monument to His life work and bowed down to worship at its shrine; we would have missed the essence of His message.

Jesus introduced the concept of the church just before He returned to His Father, giving the disciples understanding that the church was a vehicle to promote the restoration of the Kingdom of God. And He took sole responsibility to build His church, declaring that the gates of hell would not prevail against it (Matt. 16:18¬19). To the disciples He said, "And I will give unto thee the keys of the kingdom of heaven" (:19). He did not give them "keys" to the church. He gave them the keys to the Kingdom. The keys were for the establishing of His Kingdom. Even as He introduced the church, He focused the disciples' attention on the Kingdom:

> ...I will build my church; and the gates of Hades shall not prevail against it. And I will give you the keys of the kingdom of heaven, and whatever you bind on earth will be bound in heaven, and whatever you loose on earth will be loosed in heaven.
>
> **—MATTHEW 16:19**

This spiritual authority was given to believers, not to focus on being occupied managing other church members, but to learn to extend God's reign throughout the earth, bringing the will of God to earth as He originally intended. In no way does this understanding of the Kingdom diminish the importance of the church or our inheritance as children of God. On the contrary, it reveals our divine purpose and makes possible the fulfillment of our eternal destiny for every believer. The church is the vehicle through which the Kingdom can be extended. Despite all the failures and weaknesses of His church, God does not have any other plan to extend His Kingdom on the earth. The church is the body of Christ through which the message of and power of the Kingdom will be proclaimed to the whole world.

The church is the vehicle through which the Kingdom can be extended.

It is imperative that we understand that the church is not an end in itself. This can lead to self-serving. Building a big, successful church with prestige and popularity is not the goal.

The Kingdom of God—its priority, principles, purpose, values, and lifestyle—is the ultimate purpose of God on the earth. Relative to that divine purpose, the church is the most important medium of extending the Kingdom; that is its mandate as taught in the scriptures.

THE ABSOLUTISM OF THE KINGDOM; THE RELEVANCE OF THE CHURCH

To clarify the role of the church as the vehicle to extend the Kingdom of God on the earth, we must understand the scriptures that teach the Kingdom is Absolute while the church is relative. That is, the ultimate will of God resides in His domain, the Kingdom of God. The church reflects His will. This understanding will clarify the relationship of the church and the Kingdom.

The Truth of the Kingdom

Jesus declared: "I am the way, the truth, and the life: no man cometh unto the Father, but by me" (Jn. 14:6). He came to restore the Kingdom of His Father to the earth, as we have discussed. The Kingdom of God is where we find truth and life. Jesus is the King and we are transferred to His Kingdom as we come to the Father. That is why we must be born again by the Spirit of God to enter the Kingdom, to become citizens of the Kingdom. The Holy Spirit comes into us and restores us to relationship with God, teaching us to obey the principles of the Kingdom and live the Kingdom lifestyle that reflects the character of God.

It is then that we discover our citizenship as the church, the body of Christ (1 Cor. 12:27). As born again believers, we are birthed into the church where we can be nurtured in the life of the Kingdom. As we learn the ways of the Kingdom, our thinking is transformed and we are filled with the passion of God for the expansion of His Kingdom, bringing others into the Kingdom and extending the principles of the Kingdom into all spheres of society. There we are to be equipped to discover our own destiny, our promised land, where we will extend His reign throughout the earth, extending the domain of His Kingdom.

The entire New Testament is filled with the principles of the Kingdom, teaching us to love one another and to reflect the love of God in all we do. The apostle Paul declares: "The kingdom of God is not meat or drink, but righteousness, peace, and joy in the Holy Ghost" (Rom. 14:17). When Jesus gave His disciples the keys to the Kingdom, He gave them power to unlock the spiritual realities of the Kingdom lifestyle God intended mankind to enjoy from the beginning of creation. Focusing on extending the Kingdom of God results in fulfilling eternal destiny, taking dominion over the earth as Adam and Eve were instructed to do.

The Role of the Church

According to the scriptures, the church is the pillar and support of the truth—which is the Kingdom of God:

> These things write I unto thee...that thou mayest know how thou oughtest to behave thyself in the house of God, which is the church of the living God, the pillar and support of the truth
> **—1 TIMOTHY 3:14–15 NAS**

Jesus is the Truth; He is the embodiment of the Kingdom of God, the King Himself. He is the Head of His body, the church. Our role as believers is to embody the truth of His Kingdom and disseminate it throughout the earth.

The apostle Paul describes the church as the pillar and support of the truth. So the Kingdom of God is the Truth; the church is the pillar and support of the truth. The truth the church holds is a reflection of the truth of God. This clarifies the role of the church as being relative to the Kingdom of God, which is absolute. God is counting on the church, the body of Christ on the earth, to extend the domain of King Jesus.

Jesus is the Truth; The Church is the pillar and support of the truth.

A pillar upholds the weight of the edifice to which it is attached. Society is to be upheld by the truth of the Kingdom, which is resident in the church because we have the Spirit of Truth. So if the church loses its influence and voice in the society, the pillar collapses and consequently the moral fabric of our culture collapses. The eternal values that God intended to motivate the community to health and well-being disintegrates. Even the economy is affected negatively when truth is not upheld. If the church loses its ability to establish truth as the pillar upon which society rests, every sphere of life will experience deterioration and destruction. Let's review again the seven major spheres of life:

1. Spiritual/Social
2. Government/Politics
3. Business/Economy
4. Education/Science
5. Media
6. Culture/Entertainment

As the foundation and the pillar of the truth of the Kingdom of God, the church is responsible to penetrate every sphere of society. Like leaven, it is to permeate every part of our culture, transforming it to reflect the values, principles, and lifestyle of the Kingdom, bringing light into the darkness of a godless society.

Why has much of Christendom not embraced this awesome responsibility? When people don't know the purpose for which a thing is created, they abuse it. Because the purpose of the church has been misunderstood, the church has become powerless to subdue the earth by extending the domain of Christ. In too many instances, the church has become self-serving and in doing so the church has actually brought reproach to Christ, the King.

Many leaders of the church in today's society have redefined the purpose of the church. Rather than to build an organism centered on God's purposes, they are building an organization centered on their own people, to make people feel good about themselves, to meet their needs, and to satisfy the agenda of the pastor. This is in stark contrast to a living, breathing organism that moves in harmony with one purpose—to extend life from God throughout planet earth.

The church is ordained to pronounce and proclaim the truth of the Kingdom everywhere. It stands to defend those Biblical truths and manifest their reality throughout the earth. The church is not the truth; but it is a reflection of truth; it is God's organism destined to propagate the truth. This reality testifies to the absolutism of the Kingdom and the relativity of the church as well.

The Biblical purpose for the church, as we have mentioned, is to release the truth of God into all spheres of society, to disseminate the virtues of God into the earth, to uphold the truth of God and to work to bring His will to every area of life. When we realize the purpose for the church is to establish the truth of the Kingdom, we understand that the church is not the Kingdom, but a part of the Kingdom, citizens of the Kingdom with a most important role to play. Viewing the church as an end in itself becomes a man-centered view; the church is a vehicle to propagate the truth of the Kingdom of God.

There are Christians in every walk of life, regardless of their church training, who have discovered their God-given mandate and are walking in this truth of extending the Kingdom in their sphere of life. One National Football League star has made a tremendous impact by using his fame as a platform to reach multitudes of youth and others with the testimony of his faith in Christ. Aeneas Williams, who played for the Arizona Cardinals and St. Louis Rams before retiring, appeared in eight Pro Bowls.

During his football career, Williams earned a reputation as a quiet leader who professed a deep Christian faith. In the locker room, teammates often sought him out to help them put things in perspective. He now serves as pastor of a church he and his wife founded in suburban St. Louis, Missouri. His approach to pastoring is summed up in his stated goal: "The hope is that each person who attends has a personal relationship with the Lord that's practical and that they're able to take that relationship and share it with someone else".

THE SPIRIT OF THE KINGDOM

The Kingdom of God is more than principles and values based in the truth of the Kingdom. The Kingdom is also reflected in the Spirit of Christ. When you are born again, receiving Christ as Savior, the Holy Spirit quickens your spirit, making you alive to God. Your ultimate destination is heaven, but the purpose for which you were born is to fulfill God's purposes on earth. God's presence dwells in you by His Spirit, restoring His glory throughout the earth, that glory that was lost because of sin.

As the scriptures teach, it is "Christ in you the hope of glory" (Col. 1:27). The glory of God is restored to earth through redeemed believers who embrace the principles and values of the Kingdom and show forth the Spirit of Christ everywhere they go, spreading the salvation experience with others.

The Spirit of the Kingdom is reflected in grace; the principles of the Kingdom are revealed in truth. The apostle John wrote of Christ:

> And the Word was made flesh, and dwelt among us, (and we beheld his glory, the glory as of the only begotten of the Father,) full of grace and truth. And of his fullness have all we received, and grace for grace. For the law was given by Moses, but grace and truth came by Jesus Christ.
>
> **—JOHN 1:14–17**

Both grace and truth must dwell in you. Legalism, the practice of principles without grace, becomes an oppressive, religious burden, such as that which the Pharisees placed upon the people of Israel. And grace, when devoid of the principles of the Kingdom can become license and unwittingly condone unrighteousness, negating the truth of the Kingdom.

However, where the principles of the Kingdom are practiced, even among non-believers, they help to establish a society upon truth and righteousness. For example, a society that adopts the Kingdom value of honesty as a standard of living will be less vulnerable to stealing, fraud, or other dishonest practices. They will tend to trust each other and enjoy peace in their relationships, their businesses and community living. These principles of righteousness lead them to salvation. "The law of the Lord is perfect, converting the soul." Through receiving the grace of God for salvation, they are able to escape the consequences of wrong doing in hell. As those who have received the grace of

God for salvation, we can bring the Kingdom value of honesty to permeate society contributing to its peace. Kingdom principles work for all who embrace them and to whatever degree they embrace them.

Both grace and truth must dwell in you for eternal life to be yours

---

THE SCOPE OF THE KINGDOM

The fact that the principles of the Kingdom work in unbelievers as well as believers also illustrates the absolutism of the Kingdom. The benefits of the Kingdom do not belong only to the church or the Christian faith. Let me explain. Earlier, I referred to the fact that all of humanity is "wired for the Kingdom." The laws and principles of the Kingdom are imprinted in the "DNA" of our being. For that reason, the Kingdom of God encompasses governments and societal systems and entire cultures. To whatever degree a society comes under the rule—the dominion—of the principles of the Kingdom of God, His righteousness will be reflected in that society.

For example, a society where marriage is sacred and divorce is not encouraged will enjoy the Kingdom benefit of strong families. Marriage is a Kingdom value and a principle for righteous relationships. Even a society that does not know or adhere to the Christian faith will reap the blessing of this Kingdom value. They will know the order in family relationships that God intended to characterize His Kingdom. The truths of the Kingdom, while they can be violated, cannot be broken; they reward the person or society that embraces them and penalize those who attempt to overrule them

In that regard, the Kingdom of God cannot be monopolized,

either by the church or any person. Too often, the church has presumed that the benefits of the Kingdom belongs only to it, is represented only by it, and is characterized by its actions, attitudes and agenda. In this way, the church has tried to monopolize the Kingdom much like the Pharisees did in Israel during Jesus' ministry. They rewarded and penalized people according to their religious creed, their interpretation of the scriptures, their dogma and cultural expressions of worship. Jesus' indictment against them was powerful:

> Woe unto you, scribes and Pharisees, hypocrites! For ye shut up the kingdom of heaven against me: for ye neither go in yourselves, neither suffer ye them that are entering to go in.
>
> **—MATTHEW 23:13**

Because the DNA of all humanity is wired for the Kingdom, the scope of the Kingdom of God is greater than the church. The church does not have a monopoly on the Kingdom of God. The principles of the Kingdom are absolute, transcending society, religious orders, and all of humanity. In this sense also, the church is relative to the Kingdom; it is the vehicle entrusted to extend the principles and values of the Kingdom on the earth. The purpose of the church is to cultivate a lifestyle of redeemed people who embrace Kingdom principles and make their priority to extend God's reign across the earth, to the glory of its rightful Lord and King, Jesus Christ.

The church does not have a monopoly on the Kingdom of God.

If the church does not understand and properly define the

Kingdom and understand its divinely ordained relationship to that Kingdom, it cannot function in its purpose to extend the Kingdom of God on earth. For that reason there is such a plethora of organizations called "churches", doing their own thing, promoting their own causes, and ultimately deceiving people with their religious dogmas. Knowingly or unknowingly they are shutting up the Kingdom to people who may be sincerely seeking to know God.

The Believers Mandate

The dream of God is for the values and principles of the Kingdom of God to reign on the earth through the jewel of His creation, mankind, made in His image. To that end He sent Jesus to restore us to the Kingdom, teaching us its principles, living the lifestyle of the Kingdom, and then sacrificing His life on Calvary to purchase our redemption and entry into the Kingdom as citizens.

The church has often done well in presenting the gospel of salvation through Christ alone to unbelievers. However, it has not always presented the mandate of the scriptures regarding the Kingdom. That divine mandate is that every believer works to extend the Kingdom of God throughout the earth, living a lifestyle that is motivated to demonstrate the principles and values of the Kingdom in their personal life and promised land - their sphere of life.

For example in Kyiv the believers have been well taught that the only reason they are alive is to accomplish a certain mission for which God created them. So after people are born again, their primary assignment and pursuit is not to get a good job that pays well, or try to resolve all their life problems. They do not live for personal success, but rather to find out what God has sent them to the earth to do and to pursue the fulfillment of it.

Believers in Kyiv are busy with this divine pursuit praying and seeking what assignment they are supposed to carry out on the earth.

A very touching example is that of, "Life Without Justification" foundation and club. It centers on the story of a young man named Valodya who had become paralyzed due to the abuse of drugs. Having spent years in bed, and making several attempts to commit suicide, he said, "I just wanted to die. I feared being a physically challenged person meant that my life was worth nothing. He was brought to Pastor Roman's church and ministered to through a rehabilitation center of the Embassy of God Church where he began to listen to Kingdom teaching. Even though he couldn't talk or walk, he discovered that despite his physical challenges, God still wanted him to bring forth fruit for the Kingdom and be a source of blessing to others.

Valodya started his "Life Without Justification" foundation from his sick bed and wheel chair by searching for and interacting with people through the internet. Through his encouragement to other physically challenged people like him, he has developed a network of young men and women who are also paralyzed (some can't talk, speak or stand). They have learned how to carry purpose and hope for a meaningful life to people like themselves as well as to others who do not share their physical challenges, but are filled with psychological ills—living lives full of excuses for why they cannot enjoy a purposeful, meaningful life.

When we get to heaven, our ministries are not going to be judged by how big our budget was; what size property we had or by how many church members we had in our pews – but only by how much positive influence we have brought to this needy world.

That is why the focus of the local church should not be in trying to retain as many church members active in church based programs, but rather to equip them and send them out into the world to bring the influence of the Kingdom to all spheres and areas of life multiplying the number of Kingdom citizens making a Kingdom impact. For that reason, in our church in Kyiv, I always tell my members that my primary assignment is to get rid of them, i.e. from the pews to the streets - so that they can contribute salt and light to the many needs of our society and nation.

The Kingdom Transcends All Religion.

I have explained that, even in our fallen state, the principles of the Kingdom of God are programmed into our consciousness, written on our "spiritual DNA". We are made in the image of God. Even without being restored to relationship with God through faith in Christ alone, receiving Him as Savior and Lord, the principles and values of the Kingdom seek to take dominion in our lives. They chide us, crowd into our consciences, and try to persuade us of their righteousness. Jesus described this divine influence as the work of the Holy Spirit on the earth:

> Nevertheless I tell you the truth; It is expedient for you that I go away: for if I go not away, the Comforter will not come unto you; but if I depart, I will send him unto you. And when he is come, he will reprove the world of sin, and of righteousness, and of judgment: Of sin, because they believe not on me; Of righteousness, because I go to my Father, and ye see me no more; Of judgment, because the prince of this world is judged.
> —JOHN 16: 7–11

The Holy Spirit came to reprove the "world". No one is exempt from His work. He is the divine Agent sent to establish the Kingdom of God on the earth that Jesus restored us to through His death and resurrection. The Spirit of God is not limited to a religion because the Kingdom of God is not a religion; it transcends religion. There is no salvation to be found in religion; salvation is only received through faith in Jesus Christ. And the Kingdom of God is not promoted by religion—not even "Christian religion." Let me explain.

The Kingdom of God belongs to everyone. When the church tries to "clothe" the Kingdom in religious norms, the world rejects it. Jesus did not establish a religion or denomination. He demonstrated the love and lifestyle and taught the principles of the Kingdom. Though He came to the Jewish nation, the scriptures declare that "He came unto his own, and his own received Him not" (Jn. 1:11). Jesus wept over Jerusalem as the city that killed prophets and did not receive Him as their Messiah (Matt. 23:37). Indeed, religious leaders of Israel condemned Him to death. The apostles later received the revelation that God's grace was also for the gentiles, including all nations.

The Old Testament prophesies of the gentiles (pagan nations other than Israel) coming to the light (Isa 42:6). And the New Testament records Peter's revelation of God's grace being given to them as well. He was sent to the house of Cornelius, a centurion, who sought God earnestly. Peter and his Jewish friends were astonished when the Holy Spirit was poured out on the Gentiles who gathered to hear the gospel of the Kingdom in Cornelius' house that day (Acts chapter 10).

The apostle Paul understood that religion was a barrier to the gospel of the Kingdom. In Athens, He preached to the philosophers and others concerning "THE UNKNOWN GOD" that they worshiped:

God that made the world and all things therein, seeing that he is Lord of heaven and earth, dwelleth not in temples made with hands; Neither is worshipped with men's hands, as though he needed any thing, seeing he giveth to all life, and breath, and all things; And hath made of one blood all nations of men for to dwell on all the face of the earth, and hath determined the times before appointed, and the bounds of their habitation; That they should seek the Lord, if haply they might feel after him, and find him, though he be not far from every one of us.

—ACTS 17: 24–27

Once again, in the preaching of the apostles, the truth of the Kingdom transcended race, religion, and all of mankind's tradition. It transcends culture and every godless system of government, every humanistic or atheistic tenant, and all religious values. The power of the Kingdom of God to take dominion over every false philosophy and religious order has its origin in the Creator Himself. The prayer of the apostle Paul reveals this truth:

That ye might walk worthy of the Lord unto all pleasing, being fruitful in every good work, and increasing in the knowledge of God…Who hath delivered us from the power of darkness, and hath translated us into the kingdom of his dear Son: In whom we have redemption through his blood, even the forgiveness of sins: Who is the image of the invisible God, the firstborn of every creature: For by him were all things created, that are in heaven, and that are in earth, visible and invisible, whether they be thrones, or dominions, or principalities, or powers: all things were created by him, and for him: And he is before all things, and by him all things consist.

—COLOSSIANS 1: 9–10, 13–17

Pre-eminence of the Kingdom Transcends False Religions.

It is clear from these and other scriptures, that any power that has dominion apart from God is inferior to the power of God. The power of redemption through Christ transcends the power of world religions and every other power of darkness that blinds the eyes of men and women from the truth of the Kingdom of God.

A Muslim is a Muslim because of religious teaching and cultural traditions. He is a Muslim in his mindset, but he was created in the image of God. Buddhism, Atheism, Humanism, and every other "religious" mindset is subject to the laws of the Kingdom. Because the laws of the Kingdom of God are written into our "DNA", preaching those principles of the Kingdom transcends their religious dogma. The power of truth breaks the power of darkness in their religious mindset. Then they are free to receive Christ as the Way, the Truth, and the Life and be born again.

Some have asked me, how would I preach the Kingdom of God in western nations? I tell them I have the key that will turn a country around in 5 years. Islamists, Buddhists, and Muslims alike would accept my preaching. All would accept the teaching of the principles of national transformation that are working for us in Ukraine. As they embrace these principles, which are universal, society can be transformed and the way prepared for the truth of Christ to be preached.

For example, one of the lessons for national transformation I teach is that a country does not become great by virtue of their wealth. The greatness of a country is established, instead, by the wealth of their values. Greatness is not a result of a country's wealth of natural resources. If that were the case, African countries would be the greatest nations of the world. They are rich in minerals, precious stones, gold, silver, and other natural resources. But because of their value systems, graft, stealing, dishonesty, corruption in government, and greed rule their societies. These countries are doomed to failure, poverty, and smallness. Their wealth is stolen, the people are deceived, and there is no way forward for development of greatness as a nation.

What changes a nation is the truth of the Word of God working by the Spirit of God. This truth involves the teachings of Jesus regarding the Principles of the Kingdom of God. If we will preach not religion or Christian experience, but rather the truth of the Word of God, and allow the Spirit of the Lord to work, then we will discover that Kingdom principles work everywhere!

On the other hand, unbelievers resist religiosity, even the Christian religion. This reality reveals the wisdom behind our using a lot of Non-Profit Organizations in our country and others. In this way we are not preaching religion to the world. Instead we are showing the love of God and declaring and extending the Principles of the Kingdom there, believing the Spirit of God to do the transformation. This Biblical approach to evangelism explains why we have the astounding results that we do in Ukraine.

The greatness of a country is established by the wealth of their values.

When a society is established in the Biblical values of dignity, honesty, hard work, kindness, generosity, and benevolent government rule—all principles of the Kingdom of God—it will flourish economically and in every way. When those values are prevalent in a society, even if it is pagan and serving a false religion, the principles of the Kingdom of God will work for them to establish a peaceful society. Choosing to abide by Kingdom values and principles, even if they are not Christians, will bring the reward inherent to those principles. This prepares people to understand salvation; that which they need to be saved from and that which they need to be saved to.

There are nations that have higher economic standards and lower crime rates than America because their moral standards are higher than those of America. Other countries that have more natural resources of oil, gold, etc., without the necessary principles and values in their culture that will establish them, are riddled with crime, poverty, disease, and death.

Someone asked why my country, which has a large population of praying Christians as well as tremendous natural resources, has not achieved greater development or success as a nation. Christian leaders answer that question by saying that they need to pray more. You will have to visit Nigeria to understand that the Christians in my nation pray more than almost any other country where I have visited. They pray intensely, loudly, and long. They gather for all night prayer meetings and earnestly seek God together.

But nations don't develop as a result of prayer unless they also embrace the principles of the Kingdom as well. For example, stealing is a national sin in my country. Even Christians will leave a prayer meeting and go out and steal; they sometimes steal something valuable laying around in the prayer meeting. Until the Kingdom principles of honesty, integrity, and hard work become the lifestyle of Christians, my nation cannot prosper. And the church that is not living the principles of the Kingdom is not fulfilling its purpose to extend God's domain into society through the power of truth and love. Prayer alone cannot prevail over sinful lifestyles.

Religion does not promote the Kingdom.

Religion has never been an honest broker for promoting the principles of the Kingdom. For example, there was a time that some in the American church preached that only white people could be born again. Black people could not become Christians. Today, that same faulty rhetoric is often directed toward Arabs; they could never come to Christ to receive salvation. That religious mindset shuts up the Kingdom to others. Whether you are Arab or Muslim or Atheist or embrace any other religious philosophy, you can be regenerated by the Spirit of Christ and embrace the lifestyle of the Kingdom of God; you can become a Kingdom citizen by receiving the truth of salvation through faith in Jesus.

It is this understanding that the power of the Kingdom transcends religion that has motivated our church in Ukraine to embrace the whole world and every culture. We approach the world mindsets with principles and values of the Kingdom of God. As they accept them, the way is prepared to bring them to Christ, the King. We are not supposed to preach our church or religion; we are to present the Kingdom and the King to all who walk in darkness.

I am accepted by people from every religion because I bring the principles and life of the Kingdom, which everyone can see the benefit of embracing. This approach opens the door to people who would not listen to your "religious creed". The Kingdom of God supersedes all forms of man made religion. It has the inherent power to penetrate and overcome religious mindsets.

Instead of talking in religious phrases and spouting religious doctrines, demonstrate the love of the Kingdom, the humility and honesty of the Kingdom. This is true religion, to visit people in their distress. And speak truth and Kingdom principles. Jesus brought the Kingdom principles and presented them in the power of grace. The people recognized that He taught with authority and not as the religious leaders of their day. That is where the authority resides—in the truth of the principles demonstrated through a lifestyle filled with the grace of God.

Recently, I had an experience in Kyiv that confirms this truth. I was told that a Turkish man, a Muslim, was very desperate to see me. He had been in conversation with a group of girls in town who are members of our church. This Muslim was so impressed by the purity of life and godly principles of these ladies, he decided to come and find out for himself what kind of church was responsible for such godly virtues.

When I started talking to him, it was clear that he desired to be like one of us. However his fear was that he was a Muslim and couldn't stop being a Muslim, even though he had a desire to receive Jesus Christ into his life.

So, I told him that the essence of the gospel is not to make you stop being a Muslim. You see, when you tell a Muslim he must become a Christian, it is like saying to an African, he must become European before he can be a Christian. This is because being a Muslim is equated to their national identity as a person. In other words, an Arab sees himself as a Muslim, so to stop being a Muslim to him threatened his identity as an Arab, requiring that he should stop being an Arab!

Therefore, I explained to my Turkish friend that he doesn't need to stop being a Muslim, but that he only needs to receive Jesus Christ as His Lord and Savior and confess his sins. This he said he was willing to do.

Today, this very Turkish man, even though he still sees himself culturally as a Muslim, is one of our most active church members. He doesn't read the Koran anymore (in fact he's addicted to the Bible), and he doesn't go to the mosque anymore either. And he testifies of all kinds of miracles that Jesus is doing in his life.

Principles go before religiosity. That's why Jesus Christ didn't bring religion to the world; rather He brought a relationship with the Father that redeems the souls of men and women and restores them to the Kingdom. Religion is man reaching toward God with learned behavior and tradition; relationship with God transcends all of that.

TRUE DISCIPLES OF THE KINGDOM

Remember, it was the religious leaders of Israel who killed Jesus. They would not accept the truth or the life they saw in Christ. They rejected His principles and the values He taught. They did not embrace His lifestyle of love and compassion that condemned their self-righteous, pompous ways. Their envy of His power to heal and His influence with the people, as recognized by the pagan leader, Pilate, drove them to find ways to eliminate Him. They wanted to preserve their prestigious position in the religious community of Israel.

Such deception, based in pride and arrogance and religious dogma is still "killing" the Kingdom in today's religious world. Religious creeds are much easier to establish and self-righteous behavior is easier to model than true righteousness that comes through the humility of becoming as a little child. Jesus told His disciples: "…Except ye be converted, and become as little children, ye shall not enter into the Kingdom of heaven. Whosoever therefore shall humble himself as this little child, the same is greatest in the Kingdom of heaven" (Matt. 18:3–4).

Who qualifies to be considered true disciples in the Kingdom? It is those who can produce the fruit of the Kingdom. The character, lifestyle, motivation, behavior, and life of Christ must be exhibited through those who dwell in the Kingdom and possess it. The Kingdom of God cannot be reduced to religion, owned by the church, or even limited to a denominational doctrine. It transcends religion, politics, culture, and national borders.

True disciples of the Kingdom are those who produce the fruit of the Kingdom.

The powerful principles and laws of the Kingdom penetrate every level of society through those who have embraced them. If you call yourself Christian and do not produce the fruit of the Kingdom, you do not belong to the Kingdom; you don't deserve the Kingdom because you have not received the King. Jesus said plainly: "And he that taketh not his cross, and followeth after me, is not worthy of me. He that findeth his life shall lose it: and he that loseth his life for my sake shall find it" (Matt. 10:38–39). The cost of entering the Kingdom of God, as I mentioned, involves denying yourself, your ego and your carnal desires to embrace the King and His lifestyle of love and humility that Jesus demonstrated for us. Only in this way will you discover your destiny, your passion for promoting the Kingdom of God, and your place of influence to subdue the earth to the will of God.

There are many Christians and churches that do not produce the fruit of the Kingdom. According to the scriptures, the Kingdom will be taken from them and given to another. Jesus condemned chief priests and Pharisees who refused to embrace the Kingdom He came to restore: "Therefore say I unto you, the Kingdom of God shall be taken from you, and given to a nation bringing forth the fruits thereof" (Matt. 21:43).

NO CHURCH CAN
MONOPOLIZE THE KINGDOM

The Jews, the Christians, or any church organization cannot monopolize the Kingdom of God. The Catholic Church tried to monopolize the Kingdom of God, excluding anyone who did not follow their religious creed and become a part of their order. They established Peter as the Bishop of the only church, the universal church. But the time came in which God transcended their imposed monopoly with the truth of the Reformation.

The Kingdom is absolute and transcends every human attempt to reduce it to their creed and dogma. Throughout history, God has restored the truth of His Kingdom to those who would embrace it, choosing to live the lifestyle and allow the godly character to be formed that He demands. God demands that you produce the fruit of that Kingdom to be qualified to dwell in the Kingdom of God. Jesus said He would take the Kingdom from the Jewish nation and give it to a nation that would embrace regeneration through His sacrifice on Calvary, receive salvation through the blood He shed, and extend the lifestyle and principles of the Kingdom of God througout the earth, producing the fruit of it.

Less than a hundred years ago, Christians declared Africa to be the dark continent, the missionary "graveyard". They discouraged people from going to preach to the African people the gospel of Christ. Some consigned African nations to hell, declaring that they were involved in witchcraft and voodoo; they declared that they were not destined to be saved. Some even declared that they were created to be slaves, to be raw material for the economic well-being of others. They concluded that Africans could not be Christians; they were pagans without hope of redemption.

According to religious statistics, in Africa today Christianity is leading Islam in its growth and is growing twice as fast as Islam.

That is happening in spite of the terrible fact that in many places people who convert from Islam to Christianity do so at the risk of their lives. Also, it must be considered that the projected growth of Muslims is based on birth rate of primarily Muslim nations and on immigration in other nations. Growth of Christianity, on the other hand, is based on voluntary conversion of individuals. According to these statistics, the growth of Christianity in Europe is decreasing and North American growth remains stable, while Africa's Christian population is growing rapidly.

God is moving so powerfully by His Spirit that entire African nations are being born again, producing great churches and powerful ministers who are reaching into other nations. These pagans of yesterday are preaching the principles of the Kingdom today. That dark continent that did not deserve to hear the gospel has spawned powerful ministers who have reached into the old European continent, establishing powerful churches and transforming cities and nations with the power of the gospel. African ministers are reaching the nations that refused to give them the gospel. Many Black ministers like myself are raising great churches in Europe and other continents.

I can prophetically foresee a day when the power of God that is transforming Africa will be poured out on Muslims; they will be standing in my place preaching the gospel of Christ. The Arabs will preach the Kingdom of God. The powerful underground church in China is preaching the gospel and winning millions of souls to Christ against all odds and through great suffering.

The Kingdom belongs to anyone who embraces the King and his truth, life, and the lifestyle of the Kingdom, producing the fruit of the Kingdom. During Jesus' life, it was an accepted fact that only the nation of Israel was qualified to have the Kingdom of God. Jesus declared that they were not qualified because "the stone which the builders rejected, the same is become the head of the corner: this is the Lord's doing, and it is marvelous in our eyes" (Matt. 21:42).

The Jewish nation was the chosen people through whom the Messiah would come. But they were not worthy of the Kingdom because they rejected the Messiah when He came. They clung instead to their feeling of superiority, their "knowledge" of religious creeds. They had embraced religion and were blinded to the Messiah when He appeared. Jesus told them plainly that if they did not embrace the life of the Kingdom —Himself— and the lifestyle He demonstrated, bringing forth the fruit of the Kingdom, He would take it from them.

With sorrow of heart, I stand to prophesy, that if America is not careful, the Kingdom of God shall be taken from her and be handed to nations she has considered "mission fields". There must be an embracing of the lifestyle, values, and principles of the Kingdom, promoting them in the educational, political, economic, and every other sphere of society for the blessing of God to rest upon a nation. The church is responsible to penetrate society with the Kingdom truth and transform it by establishing its principles as the governing force—advancing the domain of the King and bringing the will of God to earth.

However, most of the statistics relating to the American church reveal its increasing ineffectiveness to exert a positive influence on today's culture. They tell us that nearly 50% of Americans have no church home. In the 1980's, membership in the church had dropped almost 10%; in the 1990s it worsened by another 12% drop. And now, over halfway through the second decade of the 21st century, the figures are dropping even more. The United States Census Bureau reported the following:

- Every year more than 4000 churches close their doors compared to just over 1000 new church starts.
- Every year, 2.7 million church members fall into inactivity.

- The United States now ranks third (3rd) following China and India in the number of people who are not professing Christians; in other words, the U.S. is becoming an ever increasing "un-reached people group."
- 20.5% of Americans "frequently" attended church in 1995. 18.0% of Americans "frequently" attended in church in 2002. It is predicted that, by extrapolating the data, these figures will drop to 15% of Americans in attendance at a church by 2025, with a continuing downward trend after that.
- Statistics from Barna Research reported recently that perhaps 50% of people who go to a church are not Christians. [Dr. Richard J. Krejcir, "Statistics and Reasons for Church Decline", found at Schaeffer Inistitute.
- Callout: If America is not careful, the Kingdom of God shall be taken from her.

The Kingdom does not belong to a race of people, a nation, to Christians, or any particular "brand" of church. They can embrace the Kingdom and demonstrate its pre-eminence, but not exclusively. The Kingdom rules through divine laws that apply to every person. It belongs to those who are qualified by faith to inherit the Kingdom, regardless of race, religion, educational status, or economic position. Those who will be trusted with the life of the Kingdom of God are those who are ready to produce the fruit of this Kingdom. That fruit includes righteousness, holiness, integrity, love, forgiveness, longsuffering, humility, and signs and wonders. All of the divine attributes that Christ demonstrated and the New Testament teaches are at the disposal of those who choose to embrace the pre-eminence of the King and entry into his Kingdom. They will promote its dominion on the earth and be a part of the answer to God's heartbeat—"Thy kingdom come. Thy will be done on earth as it is in heaven."

ETERNALITY OF THE KINGDOM

Another indication that the Kingdom of God is absolute is that it is everlasting. Churches, denominations, and movements all come and go. That is clear from even a cursory reading of church history. Great revivals that resulted in thousands of converts to Christianity, involved powerful signs and wonders, and spawned great denominations, have faded into antiquity, leaving behind one more religious organization. New churches in every generation spring up around those who seek first the Kingdom of God and His righteousness and bring revival to a community, a city, or a nation.

As a vehicle for spreading the gospel of the Kingdom, the church is only as effective as its leadership and each believer who determines to live the principles and lifestyle of the Kingdom. When the church preaches only the gospel of salvation without understanding the importance of extending the Kingdom by presenting the principles of the Kingdom, it has no social relevance; it cannot extend the Kingdom throughout the earth.

It is imperative that believers do not give their lives to service of a church instead of the church extending the Kingdom. It may seem sincerely noble to do so. Giving your life to extending the Kingdom is what will bring forth everlasting fruit and bring the will of God to earth. Embracing Christ and the principles of the Kingdom will make you relevant and capable of bringing social change and transformation.

DIVINE INHERITANCE

Another indication of the absolutism of the Kingdom is the divine inheritance promised to believers. Believers who embrace the Kingdom reality do not inherit the church. The church is Jesus' inheritance. The inheritance of the church is the Kingdom. Jesus promised that we will inherit the Kingdom prepared from the foundation of the world:

> When the Son of man shall come in his glory, and all the holy angels with him, then shall he sit upon the throne of his glory: And before him shall be gathered all nations: and he shall separate them one from another, as a shepherd divideth his sheep from the goats: And he shall set the sheep on his right hand, but the goats on the left. Then shall the King say unto them on his right hand, Come, ye blessed of my Father, inherit the kingdom prepared for you from the foundation of the world.
> **—MATTHEW 25:31–34KJV (EMPHASIS ADDED)**

When Christ returns, He sets the nations before Him and judges them according to this criteria of the lifestyle of the Kingdom:

> For I was an hungred, and ye gave me meat: I was thirsty, and ye gave me drink: I was a stranger, and ye took me in: Naked, and ye clothed me: I was sick, and ye visited me: I was in prison, and ye came unto me. Then shall the righteous answer him, saying, Lord, when saw we thee an hungred, and fed thee? Or thirsty, and gave thee drink? When saw we thee a stranger, and took thee in? or naked, and clothed thee? Or when saw

we thee sick, or in prison, and came unto thee? And the King shall answer and say unto them, Verily I say unto you, Inasmuch as ye have done it unto one of the least of these my brethren, ye have done it unto me.

—MATTHEW 25: 35–40KJV

While the ministry of the church is relevant only for the earth, the Kingdom is the reality of both heaven and earth. When the church gets to heaven she will be the bride of Christ. This reality reveals not only the preciousness of the church to Her Lord, but also indicates the divine character that the church is to demonstrate on the earth.

The apostle Paul used the analogy of the body of Christ to describe the church. He said that Christ is the Head of the Body, His church. In the natural, the head or brain determines every thought, action, attitude, and response of the body. It cannot function in life apart from the direction and empowerment of the head. The church that will inherit the Kingdom of God must be completely surrendered to the mandates of the gospel of the Kingdom. This may be the most insightful revelation of the divine nature and lifestyle that the church must exhibit on the earth to produce the fruit of the Kingdom.

Jesus' life demonstrated how the lifestyle of the Kingdom reached out to every sphere of society where there were hurting, needy people: prisoners, hungry, thirsty, lonely strangers, sick and poor. And His parable about feeding the hungry revealed that those disciples who had demonstrated the love and compassion of the Kingdom on the earth would inherit the heavenly Kingdom prepared for them from the foundation of the world. The reward for serving God through the vehicle of the church—the body of Christ—is to inherit the Kingdom.

As a pastor, I have learned that church members come and

go, die, disappoint, and break a pastor's heart. I cannot look to my members for my reward; my reward is the Kingdom which cannot be shaken. It is important for pastors to be faithful shepherds to the church, raise people up to be equipped to extend the Kingdom throughout the earth. But it is equally important not to become attached to the church that you can see in front of you; it is not the end of your labor. Get your heart attached to God Himself, His values and principles and His heartbeat to spread the Kingdom in the whole earth. Inspire, instruct, and empower believers to live and demonstrate the transforming power of the Kingdom, reaching out to every sphere of life with the good news of the gospel.

For all who will heed the message of the Kingdom, learning to live its reality and spread its influence, the power of the Kingdom will be demonstrated through them. Because Jesus had only one purpose, to do God's will, to restore the Kingdom of God to the earth, the power of the Holy Spirit was given to Him without measure (Jn. 3:34). He did only what He saw His Father doing (Jn. 5:19).

When believers surrender completely to the pre-eminence of God and his rule in extending the Kingdom, they will experience the supernatural power of the Kingdom in ways they did not think possible. As we prepare to discuss the power of the Kingdom in the next chapter, I invite you to pray this prayer with me:

KINGDOM PRAYER

Heavenly Father, I ask you for the "zeal of thine house" to burn in my heart, filling me with a passion to extend your Kingdom as the absolute purpose of your heart. Let me be a part, in the sphere of influence you have given me, of increasing your government, your dominion, and your peace. Please wash me of erroneous concepts of your church, the purpose for which you intended it, and my destiny as a believer. I embrace the revelation of these Kingdom principles and ask you to show me how to demonstrate them in my life. Help me to focus my energies, resources, and my whole being on becoming a God-carrier, to extend your Kingdom throughout the earth. Thank you, Father, in Jesus name, amen!

KINGDOM PRINCIPLES
FROM CHAPTER 5

1. When empowered by the Spirit of God, the body of Christ is the most potent force in earth, endowed with divine authority to rule and reign according to the principles of the Kingdom of God.
2. Despite all the failures and weaknesses of His church, God does not have any other plan to extend His Kingdom on the earth.
3. The Kingdom of God is the Truth; the church is the pillar and support of the truth. This fact makes the church relative to the Kingdom.
4. The church is not the truth, it reflects the truth; it is God's organism destined to propagate the truth. This reality testifies to the absolutism of the Kingdom and the relativity of the church as well.
5. The fact that the principles of the Kingdom work in unbelievers as well as believers also illustrates the absolutism of the Kingdom.
6. The power of redemption through Christ transcends the power of world religions and every other power of darkness that blinds the eyes of men and women from the truth of the Kingdom of God.

7. The Kingdom is absolute and transcends every human attempt to reduce it to their creed, dogma or their organization. Throughout history, God has restored the truth of His Kingdom to those who would embrace it

8. God demands that you produce the fruit of that Kingdom to demonstrate that you are in the Kingdom of God

9. For all who will heed the message of the Kingdom, learning to live its reality and spread its influence, the power of the Kingdom will be demonstrated through them.

10. When believers surrender completely to the pre-eminence of the King and the principles of His Kingdom, they will experience the supernatural power of the Kingdom in ways they did not think possible.

Chapter 6

THE POWER OF THE KINGDOM

But in the last days it shall come to pass, that the mountain of the house of the LORD shall be established in the top of the mountains, and it shall be exalted above the hills; and people shall flow unto it.

—MICAH 4:1

G od never intended for the church to be disregarded, humiliated, powerless, and without influence, unable to extend the Kingdom of God throughout the earth. Before His ascension, Christ promised His disciples that they would receive divine power upon their lives:

But ye shall receive power, after that the Holy Ghost is come upon you: and ye shall be witnesses unto me both in Jerusalem, and in all Judaea, and in Samaria, and unto the uttermost part of the earth

—ACTS 1:8

God established the church on the earth as the vehicle to extend His Kingdom in the world, filling the earth with His glory and bringing it under his will, the Lordship of Christ. As the light of the world, the church is to extend the Kingdom principles of grace and truth and subdue every dark thing to advance the Kingdom of God.

God never intended for the church to be powerless.

The lives of the disciples were to be empowered to such an extent that they would be successful in carrying the gospel witness to the ends of the earth. And Jesus' promise to all who believe in Him is: "…the works that I do shall he do also; and greater works than these shall he do; because I go unto my Father (Jn. 14:12).

REDEEMING THE SPHERE OF BUSINESS

When it comes to the sphere of business, I normally teach our members that the primary purpose of business as it relates to the Kingdom of God, is not to make money. Money is only a compensation or reward for our labor. Rather, the purpose of Kingdom businesses is two-fold.

First, God designates people to go into business because He is interested in capturing that particular sphere of business. It is important to always seek the face of the Lord and find out what area of life God desires us to go into. Because the primary burden in the heart of God is to restore all things back to Himself, He sends us to those spheres of destiny to bring His glory and principles to replace the darkness there.

The second purpose of business is to subdue money and use the ungodly wealth of the world to gain eternal treasure in the Kingdom of God.

There is a man in my church named Robert. His testimony is a wonderful demonstration of empowerment to do the works of God:

Before Robert met Christ, he was owner of several casinos and was influential in the business world of Kiev. He accidentally discovered the location of the theatre that Embassy of God was renting shortly after its inception. It seemed ideal for the expansion of his business, and he inquired of the owner how much rent he would have to pay to acquire it to establish another casino. The owner told him that a church was renting it. He had heard that the church was just a small sect or cult, as it was rumored to be, and offered the theatre owner more money for the facility than he was currently receiving in rent. He learned later that the owner went to Pastor Adelaja, who was renting the theatre, and told him he would have to find another facility for his church because he was going to rent it for more money

Several years later, Robert came to Christ and began to seek God to show him his purpose in life. He took the training classes of our church, and then began to pray many nights from midnight to 6:00 a.m. for direction. However, when he would return to his business during the day, he got so involved in it that he became discouraged in his walk with the Lord. For a year, he kept praying with others many nights from midnight to 6:00 a.m. The prayer group was wonderful and prophetic words would come to encourage them. Then the next day, the reality of business would become priority again.

After a year of fasting and prayer, God began to talk to Robert about the two things that people seek after if they do not know the Lord: Money and health. The Lord began to guide him into a way to captivate people's interest and then present them with the gospel of the Kingdom. Robert started a Wellness

Center where people could come to receive free treatments and then listen to "Wellness lectures" that presented principles of the Kingdom. For paying customers, there were more benefits available in the Wellness Center, and in that way they financed the business. He trained his workers to present Kingdom principles, and they continually added more expertise and equipment to their Wellness Centers to help restore health to the people. In 2 years they have established over 250 centers in more than 20 countries and have ministered to over three million people face-to-face, presenting the gospel to them.

As pastor of the church in that theater, you might imagine I was very unhappy to be told that we would have to move our fledgling church to another location in order for an unbeliever to use it for a casino. I wrestled before God with that decision, and would not relent until I "made a deal" with God. I said, "OK, God, if I have to move this church to give an unbeliever this space, I will do it on one condition—that you save this man and make him a servant of the Kingdom. You can see how powerfully God answered my prayer from the above testimony of millions of people hearing the gospel through this businessman's Wellness Centers.

We have not even begun to tap into the power of the Kingdom that the church has at its disposal, which will transform cities and nations. Every sphere of life must be influenced by the Truth— Christ and the pillar and support of truth—the church.

PROPHECY OF THE END-TIME CHURCH

My emphasis on extending the Kingdom of God throughout the earth is what Jesus taught and demonstrated in His life and ministry. This focus on the Kingdom in no way minimizes or demeans the church, Christ's body on the earth. It only serves to extend the Biblical identity of the church and define its purpose and its goals. Emphasizing the Kingdom of God actually clarifies the eternal purpose of God for His church, empowering it to fulfill its holy mandate.

God's eternal purpose for the church must be realized in order for His Kingdom to come and His will to be done on the earth. And Christ will have a glorious church that is holy and without blemish. It will be a people who are surrendered totally to His will, extending His Kingdom on the earth. The Old Testament prophet, Micah, foretold this glorious church in the last days in all its power and glory:

> But in the last days it shall come to pass, that the mountain of the house of the LORD shall be established in the top of the mountains, and it shall be exalted above the hills; and people shall flow unto it. And many nations shall come, and say, Come, and let us go up to the mountain of the LORD, and to the house of the God of Jacob; and he will teach us of his ways, and we will walk in his paths: for the law shall go forth of Zion, and the word of the LORD from Jerusalem.
>
> **—MICAH 4:1–2**

I don't think anyone who is familiar with the scriptures would deny that we are living in the last days. It was in the last days that Micah prophesied the "mountain of the house of the LORD" would be exalted above the hills. Consider for a moment this description of the church as a mountain. What a powerful and majestic metaphor! It is impossible to disregard a mountain and when you see a mountain that is looming over the hills around it, its majestic presence grabs your attention.

Christ will have a glorious church that is without blemish.

Micah was prophetically describing the exaltation of the church in the last days. It is time for the humiliation of the church to end. Before Christ returns, He will make sure the church is no longer disregarded, taunted, and set aside from wielding its divine influence on the earth. In the New Testament, the church is linked to Mount Zion as well:

> But you have come to Mount Zion and to the city of the living God, the heavenly Jerusalem, to an innumerable company of angels, to the general assembly and church of the firstborn, who are registered in heaven, to God the Judge of all, to the spirits of just men made perfect, to Jesus the Mediator of the new covenant, and to the blood of sprinkling that speaks better things than that of Abel.
>
> **—HEBREWS 12:22–24**

Micah saw the house of the Lord exalted above all the surrounding hills. Since the church—described in the metaphor of a mountain—is an organism of born-again believers, this reference to "surrounding hills" could represent any other human or political powers on the earth. Consider some of those modern day hills of society: Wall Street, the Pentagon, the liberal media, Congress, Parliament, Dictators, False religions. There is a day coming when these "surrounding hills" will be overshadowed by the exaltation of the house of the Lord.

This prospect may seem unreasonable at present, given

the powerful influence that Wall Street and other political, educational, religious, and social institutions have at present over the lives of millions of people, including Christians. Where is the power and authority of the church in the face of challenges to the sanctity of marriage between a man and woman, to the liberty of reading the Bible and praying in our schools, to unborn babies legally murdered through abortion rights, and many other ungodly "hills" looming over society. Brazen attempts to silence the weakening voice of righteousness of the church are a regular onslaught against the presence of Mount Zion.

Yet, in the midst of the overwhelming darkness, God is raising up a people who will believe God and His Word, walk in His power and authority, and become the church that transforms the kingdom of darkness into the Kingdom of Light. God will find believers in every land, in every culture, in every nation who assert the authority given to every believer. With even one individual believer who will read this prophetic word and dare to declare, "God Almighty said it and He watches over His word to perform it" (Jer. 1:12), God can change a nation. God can bring His word to pass in a day.

UNDERSTANDING THE PROMISE

When the prophet Daniel read the prophet Jeremiah, he understood that their captivity was to have ended in 70 years. Yet, 70 years had passed and they were still captives. Why had the captivity not ended in 70 years as it had been prophesied? Daniel set himself to fast and pray for his nation to be delivered when he understood the Word of the Lord. Because no one understood the divine decree, no one had laid claim to that promise; they did not believe the word of God over their circumstances that held them captive.

God responded to His servant's earnest prayer and sent the angel Gabriel to Daniel to open his understanding of the plan of God for their deliverance. The key to the Kingdom that is paramount to walking in divine power on the earth is understanding, which we will discuss.

The imminent release from captivity of the children of Israel seemed impossible when viewing their circumstances. But when one man sought God for His promise to be fulfilled, God had to honor His Word. It is time for the church to decide whose report to believe. Will we accept the godless philosophies and practices of government, social institutions, and economic powers? Or will we enforce the principles, values, and virtues of the Kingdom of God on the earth? Our choice will determine how we walk in the divine power of the Kingdom of God.

There will be those who dare to agree with the Word of God that the mountain of the house of God will be more exalted than any other institution. As they lift up the name of the Lord Jesus, the Spirit of God will begin to descend in power. God will begin to do such miraculous works through the church that all the "hills" of the world will have to take notice. And Mount Zion will take pre-eminence over them.

MY PERSONAL VISION

As a young man in Ukraine, I embraced the truth of Micah's prophetic picture of the church. I saw my destiny in the promise that the authority of the church would be more respected than any other institution, no matter how influential. When I began to teach this message of the pre-eminence of the Kingdom a number of years ago, I was reaching a small, ordinary, poor group of people. Yet, I was prophesying, according to the Word of God, what He intended for His church in the entire nation of

Ukraine.

As God enlarged my understanding of the purpose of the church to release the power of the Kingdom, I told God I would pay the price. I surrendered to Him to go all the way, do anything required, fast and pray and seek His face, so that the church He loves would become the glorious church He ordained it to be. I determined to seek Him until the authority of His house would not lag behind any other authority on earth.

You probably cannot imagine how despised Africans are in Ukraine. As a black man from Nigeria, I was the least of candidates to establish His glorious church in that land. With the lack of authority the Christian church had there already, it seemed as if God was going to mess it up more by calling me, a black man in Ukraine, to establish His church.

But God is no respecter of persons. He has respect only for faith. Race does not help or hinder the matter. What matters is that a person believes the Word of God. If you believe God and want to extend His authority and glory throughout the earth; if you are ready to pay the price of seeking Him alone, God will release His power and authority through you.

Today, the testimony of more than 25,000 members of the Embassy of God Church reverberates the truth that God has restored the respect for His church throughout the entire nation of Ukraine. One sociological poll taken showed that for 8 years running the most respected authority in our nation is the church. That poll compared the church to the president, parliament, media, military, and other influential institutions, "the surrounding hills"; Mount Zion has prevailed.

We are still in the process of exalting the mountain of the Lord over every "hill" of influence in our nation. We will not stop until we bring the respect of God's Kingdom to every sphere of life, so that God's name will be glorified. We are going to continue to subdue the earth and make a statement in the political arena, in entertainment and media, education, arts and culture, business and education, and the sports world. As believers understand their destiny and determine to take dominion over their "promised land", they will cause their "hill" of society to bow in respect for God's church.

I am preaching this message of the Kingdom in America because I believe it is time to restore the glory of the King and the authority of Kingdom back to America. To that end, I am encouraging believers to put their faith in God to do it. It is an insult to live in a country that has professed to be a Christian nation and witness the powerlessness and lack of influence the church is having on society at large. Multitudes of Americans are actually despising the church and have no respect for it. With a large percentage of Americans claiming to be born again Christians, why should a smaller number of liberals, homosexuals, and atheists mock the Kingdom values promoted by the church? And even try to gain ungodly influence within the church itself?

In Ukraine where less than 5% of people are born-again Christians, yet the nation itself has great respect for the church. From top levels of government, to educational institutions and business enterprises, to the arena of sports and entertainment, we have made our influence felt. Extending the values and principles and lifestyle of God's love is commanding respect of believers and unbelievers alike. The good that we are bringing to our society, as we subdue it to the Lordship of Christ, is releasing the power of the Kingdom into thousands of lives.

Promotion or Persecution?

I feel the pain of American Christians and the desperate onslaught of darkness they face from political institutions and other ungodly influences that mock the principles of righteousness and taunt the values of the church. Many American Christians wonder where to start to reclaim territory for God and empower the church to regain respect and authority in their society. First, you need to understand that extending the Kingdom of God may require you to suffer some persecution. Then, you must surrender to God, as I did in Ukraine, to seek Him until He shows you His plan.

I feel the pain of American Christians.

The first thing I did to gain understanding of how to bring the Kingdom of God to Ukraine was to go on a journey into God. I needed to discover Him. I needed to touch the source of His power. I knew if I could find Him, He would explain the way to me. So I preached to my people their need to seek God earnestly. I was seeking Him fervently in prayer and fasting. In His faithfulness, He gave me the master plan for "imposing" God on the culture, not just in Ukraine, but for any ungodly culture. He showed me how to establish His Kingdom principles and enforce the will and purpose of God for a nation.

During the past 12 years, we have seen the powerful influence this strategy of extending the Kingdom has had in every sphere of life in our nation. Now, even if I left Ukraine, the power mechanism that has been put into place will make it impossible for multitudes to escape the leaven of believing Christians who will exalt the church and its influence in every sphere of life.

Taking the Challenge

How can you live as a Christian and not wield the power that comes from the influence of Kingdom values, principles, and lifestyle on the culture? It is the mandate of every Christian to extend the Kingdom of God on the earth. The priority of your life as a believer and the decisions regarding your lifestyle, your career, your relationships, must reflect the glory of Christ in everything you do. Only when you make the Kingdom of God your goal, the will of God your passion, and the glory of God your first love, will you discover your personal destiny, the reason you were born.

Yet, it seems in America, the mindset in the church is not willing to take the challenge of subduing your community and the nation to the reign and rule of God, working to see His will done on earth as it is in heaven. Everyone seems intent on doing their own thing; there is no understanding of the goal to submit the kingdoms of the earth to God's reign and to the Lordship of Christ. Church-life is separated from and not relevant to personal vocation, choices, and other lifestyle goals. While the church is expected to meet the needs of a believer and help to make them a better, more Christ-like person, there is little expectation that it should impact the lives of individuals, bringing them into the Kingdom and society as a whole by extending throughout society the principles of the Kingdom.

There seems to be little sense of responsibility among believers for taking the territory where they are laboring and restoring it to the guidance of Kingdom principles. And there is less faith that individual believers can have a godly impact on an entire sphere of life that they have chosen as a vocation. Believers "work for a living" instead of living for the Kingdom purposes, having the expectation that the power of God will transform their community through their influence. Without this conviction, there seems to be little interest or faith for reaching their own nation or the nations of the world with the gospel of the Kingdom.

In the testimony of Robert, mentioned earlier, who owned a successful casino business before he came to Christ, he received understanding through prayer that God wanted to use him to build Wellness Centers. So he began to build wellness centers all over Ukraine. In 3 years he has managed to build over 700 wellness centers, and 600 small wellness rooms. The philosophy of his business is to touch as many people as possible with the gospel through love and ministry.

These wellness centers provide free diagnosis and free treatment for as many as would like to receive it; providing services in diagnosis and massage and then offering clients to purchase the health equipment for their homes. At first, the nation couldn't believe this service was real, but very soon each one of the 700 centers had people lining up from as early as 5 o'clock in the morning to receive treatment before they would go to work. This goes on all day until 7 o'clock in the evening when the center finally closes.

The workers of these wellness centers don't just minister physical healing, but also minister what they call "Total Wellness" to people by reaching out for physical, mental and spiritual wellness. When spiritual wholeness is addressed, they share the gospel with their visitors. This is a brilliant way of sharing the gospel without imposing faith on people. Using this strategy of Kingdom expansion, there are over 5 million people who have been touched in the first 4 years of the company's existence. As a result, five thousand people have joined the church with over 50,000 giving their lives to Christ.

As we mentioned, offering additional services and selling health equipment to their clients finances these centers. Many clients prefer to continue private treatment, so they buy health equipment for their homes. As it turns out, these sales are more than enough to cover the entire overhead of the centers and to make a profit for the owners of the business as well.

This successful business venture shows the clear advantage of releasing members of your church to take the Kingdom message out from behind the 4 walls of the church and into all spheres of society. It is the understanding of this Kingdom message that prompted Robert and his business colleagues to find a means of using their business initiative to bring the redemptive influence of the Kingdom into the area of wealth, while also subduing the god of mammon to the profit of God's Kingdom.

Christians have little expectation of impacting society as a whole.

Yet, the prophet describes an end-time church that is filled with power and impacting nations: "…Many nations shall come, and say, Come, and let us go up to the mountain of the LORD" (Mic. 4:2). So dramatic is the impact of Mount Zion, the house of Jacob, that nations declare their need to come to it to be taught the ways of God and to walk in his paths (:2). The prophet declares that this end-time revival is a direct result of the law going forth from Zion and the word of the Lord from Jerusalem (:2).

Disappointment in My Home Country

I remember when I returned to Nigeria after being away from my home country for 20 years. I had heard good reports about a move of God there with many miracles and signs taking place. So, I took one of the ministers from my church in Ukraine with me to see what God was doing in my home country. We were there for 5 weeks. At the end of the 4th week, my companion said he would never come back to Africa.

I was stunned. He looked at me and said, "I hope you will not follow their example for our church in Ukraine. The gospel you preach is different from what they are preaching here. After visiting several African churches, I have not heard one message telling me about how to know God, Who He is, and how to learn His ways. Every message is centered on getting your miracle today and being blessed. I just want to know God. In these meetings, we hear about all the promises for the people; I just want to know God. They tell them to bring an offering and I will be blessed. I don't need blessings; I need to discover God. I am hungry to know Him. Don't preach to me about prosperity and healing; tell me about Him."

When that minister returned to Ukraine, he left our church for 3 years because he was afraid I would change my message and start preaching what my Nigerian brothers were teaching as the gospel. Finally, after all that time, he came back. He was satisfied that the gospel of the Kingdom was still being preached in our church.

The harvest of nations and the end-time revival is not for egocentric or selfish people who are "using" God for their benefit. This harvest will be for those who are hungry for God, wanting to learn His ways and to walk in His paths. They will love God, reflect His character, carry His image to the whole earth, surrender to His will and allow His character to draw people to Himself. There is nothing more attractive than the love of God flowing out of a heart that is totally surrendered to God's will.

MANIFESTING THE POWER OF THE KINGDOM

When the people of God begin to reflect the virtues of the Kingdom in their speech and exhibit the passion for the Kingdom in their actions and priorities, they will restore the earth to the reign of God, individuals to the King and society to the principles of the Kingdom. Out of Zion that divine authority will begin to come forth with the principles, values, and virtues— the law of God.

When the church teaches this gospel of the Kingdom, it will equip believers to carry the authority of that Kingdom into the society. They will begin extending its righteousness in their personal sphere of influence. And other people will follow them, men and women who live by principle in business; people will follow. In politics, people will follow. Unlocking the divine power of the principles of the Kingdom —honesty, integrity, compassion, generosity, and kindness—people of principle can bring the laws of God to every sphere of life and ultimately lead the world into the knowledge of the ways of the Lord.

The glorious day will come that the prophet saw; the day will come when the glory of God covers the earth and people flow into the church from every tribe and nation. But it won't happen automatically that you wake up and people are flowing into your church from every nation. Some, like Daniel, have to understand the word of the Lord and pay a price to seek God for its fulfillment. They will have to stand and claim this promise for the church to be exalted. If you can pay the price, it will happen for your city, in your nation.

People of principle can bring the laws of God into every sphere of life.

The church will become a mountain, established on the top of the mountains and exalted above every other hill (Mic. 4:1). The mountain of the house of the Lord in your city, in your nation, will be exalted above any other institution—and many people will flow into it.

THE APOSTLE PAUL'S SOURCE OF POWER

> For I will not dare to speak of any of those things which Christ hath not wrought by me, to make the Gentiles obedient, by word and deed, through mighty

signs and wonders, by the power of the Spirit of God; so that from Jerusalem, and round about unto Illyricum, I have fully preached the gospel of Christ.

—ROMANS 15:18–19

The apostle Paul subdued the whole continent of Asia to the Lord by the power of the gospel with signs and wonders. If we are to follow the example of Jesus and His apostles, we must be able to tap into their source of power. When we learn to walk in that divine power, we are able to subject every area to the lordship of Christ where we are to reign in life.

To extend the Kingdom of God throughout the earth today, the church must believe that this divine power is capable of giving you authority. In the business world, for example, if that is the sphere of life to which you are called, Kingdom principles can prevail. If you are called into the area of sports, know that there is a power in you by which you can take authority and be successful in that arena of sports. Your success will give you a platform to declare the Kingdom of God as the source of that success. People listen to those who demonstrate extraordinary success in their field. And when you attribute your success, as the apostle Paul did, to the power of the Spirit of God working through you, your witness will impact many lives for the Kingdom.

The power of God is not to lie dormant in you. It is not for "decoration" of you as a person. Nor is it to exalt you as if you were the source of the success it gives you in life. The power of God is to be used to subdue the earth for the Kingdom of God. It is to take back territories for the Lord Jesus Christ until the heavens and earth echo the word of God that says, "The kingdoms of this world are become the kingdoms of our Lord, and of his Christ; and he shall reign for ever and ever" (Rev. 11:15).

So any gifts and talents that He has trusted to you are meant to become instruments to conquer the earth, to take authority in that territory and reflect the glory of the Lord through your life. The scriptures declare that the earth is the Lord's and the fullness thereof; that is the divine intent for the earth, to reflect the glory of God. Through Christ's redemption, the earth is to be regained to show forth His glory. As believers, we are commissioned to work to fulfill that assignment.

Charisma Magazine placed the picture of David Tyree on the cover of an issue. In an article titled, "The Game of the Century", David tells how God was involved in his life and especially in the victory he experienced in Super Bowl XLII, in Glendale, Arizona. Wide receiver for the New York Giants, David Tyree and his team found themselves down 14 to 10 with 1 minute and 15 seconds remaining in the game. Here is David's account of what happened next:

> Eli Manning (the New York Giants' quarterback) took the snap, faded back to throw and somehow escaped a sure tackle by three defenders who were grabbing at his jersey. He got the ball away, lobbing it on a long, 32-yard pass. At the other end I was waiting—an obscure special-teams player for the Giants. I jumped, reached high and caught the ball. I wasn't able to pull it against my body, so I mashed it hard against my helmet and held on. Pass complete! Seconds later, wide receiver Plaxico Burress took another pass from Eli for a touchdown, and the Giants won the game. The new score, 17-14, flashed on the scoreboard.

After the game, the media and other professional athletes tauted Tyree's catch as the greatest play of all time. And NFL statistics show that Super Bowl XLII was the most- watched Super Bowl game in the history of the sport. According to David, the greatest blessing for him is the public platform it has given him, who was an unrecognized Giants' player, to tell everyone how God helped him to be a winner that day. He is taking this opportunity as a professional athelete role model to share his relationship with Christ with everyone who will listen—that is millions of people around the world.

The power of God is not to lie dormant in you.

EMPOWERED TO FULFILL
THE GREAT COMMISSION

The essence of the Great Commission is to go into all the world and extend the impact of the gospel message, its lifestyle, principles, values and virtues. God is not talking about your simply mentioning to someone that you love Jesus. He doesn't want you to "do your duty" to witness to others. Jesus said that He sent us into the world as the Father sent Him. And the apostle Paul described the purpose of our sending:

> To the intent that now unto the principalities and powers in heavenly places might be known by the church the manifold wisdom of God, according to the eternal purpose which he purposed in Christ Jesus our Lord"
>
> **—EPHESIANS 3:10-11**

The power the Lord has given us is to be used to perplex and beat down principalities and powers that have had dominion all over the earth. We are to extend the dominion of righteousness, peace, and joy in the Holy Ghost.

We are to become the answer to the prayer, "Thy kingdom come. Thy will be done on earth as it is in heaven." The power of God is available to you to take the will of God and bring His authority to rule the earth. The power of God enables you to suppress opposition and decree the will of God in any sphere of life to which you are called. That is what Jesus did when he walked on the earth. Everywhere He went he released and demonstrated the power of God, thereby extending the Kingdom in that place. Then He commissioned his followers to go and preach the Kingdom, heal the sick, raise the dead. Those signs are simply instruments to extending the Kingdom; they are keys that open territories and nations to the truth of the Kingdom.

DON'T PRAY FOR POWER

One of the mistakes I made as a young Christian was to pray for power for signs and wonders. I was so impressed by the men God was using around the world—men of God like Benny Hinn, T.L. Osborn, and others who demonstrated the power of God through healings and miracles in their ministries. It is possible to become so zealous for the things of the Lord that you can unknowingly do something that is unscriptural to receive them. So, I used to pray for power: "Father give me your power." I used to fast to get power. I thought that when I had that supernatural, miracle working power it would solve all the problems.

But I want to be very clear that to pray for the power of God is unscriptural. I learned from the scriptures that nowhere in the New Testament do the apostles or believers pray for power. Let me explain. When Jesus manifested the power of God, the Pharisees and the people were amazed. But Jesus accused the

Pharisees of thinking evil regarding His power:

> And, behold, they brought to him a man sick of the palsy, lying on a bed: and Jesus seeing their faith said unto the sick of the palsy; Son, be of good cheer; thy sins be forgiven thee. And, behold certain of the scribes said within themselves, this man blasphemeth. And Jesus knowing their thoughts said, wherefore think ye evil in your hearts? For whether is easier, to say, Thy sins be forgiven thee; or to say, Arise, and walk? But that ye may know that the Son of man hath power on earth to forgive sins, (then saith he to the sick of the palsy,) Arise, take up thy bed, and go into thine house.
>
> **—MATTHEW 9:2–6**

To pray for the power of God is unscriptural.

The Pharisees accused Jesus of blasphemy because He assumed the power to forgive sins. They knew that only God had that power, and they did not accept the divinity of Jesus. And Jesus, knowing their thoughts, asked them why they were thinking evil of Him.

In some Christian circles, my assertion that it is unscriptural to pray for power may be condemned in the same way the Pharisees condemned Jesus. There are many Christians who feel that their problems would all be solved if they could just receive the power of God to conquer them. I preached in another country that we were not to pray for revival and the leadership there did not receive that message. They tried to correct my theology. But I will show you Biblical that for the same reason you do not pray for power, you do not pray for revival to come. You can pray for power and for revival to come for years and it will not happen.

People who have understanding of the ways of God will simply operate in the power of God as they step out to extend the Kingdom. In this way they will bring revival to their land—without praying for it. To walk in the power of God it is not praying for power that you need; you need to exercise faith in the Word of God:

> And Jesus came and spake unto them, saying, all power is given unto me in heaven and in earth. Go ye therefore, and teach all nations, baptizing them in the name of the Father, and of the Son, and of the Holy Ghost: Teaching them to observe all things whatsoever I have commanded you: and, lo, I am with you always, even unto the end of the world. Amen.
>
> **—MATTHEW 28:18–20**

After Jesus' declared, "It is finished", and after He went to hell and took the keys of hell and death (Rev. 1:18), and was resurrected from the dead, He said, "All power is given unto me in heaven and on earth" (:18). He was still on earth when He made that declaration. It was not a declaration of the future. He told His followers that the power of the Lord to do the works that Jesus did is already here, on the earth.

To walk in the power of God you need faith in the Word of God.

He did not instruct the disciples to seek for power; he told them to seek the Kingdom and His righteousness. He told them he would give them power and to go and extend his Kingdom across the earth. They had the power that He had been given.

They were not to worry about the power to do it. His statement inferred that they would have all the power they needed because it had been given to Him if they would obey Him and go.

When we pray for divine power, we are assuming that we will receive that power from heaven. Jesus said it has already been given to me on the earth. Your part is to walk in obedience and become a God-carrier. Later, the apostle Paul would describe our source of power as "Christ in you, the hope of glory" (Col.1:27).

POWER COMES THROUGH
DIVINE REVELATION

Earlier, when Jesus addressed the Pharisees concerning their evil thoughts, He told them why He had declared the paralyzed man's sins forgiven: "...that ye may know that the Son of man hath power on earth to forgive sins..." (Matt. 9:6).

Whether it is a question of divine power or a desire for revival, or any other question we might present to the Father, the key to receiving an answer lies in spiritual revelation of the ways of God. Jesus was giving more than a healing to a paralyzed man that day. He was revealing hidden knowledge of Who He was and the power that was resident in Him to forgive sin. He wanted people to know that He had brought the power of God to earth.

God knows that the problem with people lies in what they know, or perhaps more accurately, what they don't know. Your whole life in the Kingdom of God is limited by what you know; the exploits you do are limited by your revelation of God. No man can do more than what he knows. You are limited by your knowledge of the Lord and of the principles of His Kingdom. You will never achieve spiritual victories that you do not know are possible. So Jesus was opening the minds of the people by knowledge and revelation.

The reason the Pharisees were thinking evil regarding Jesus, accusing Him of blasphemy, is that they lacked knowledge of Who He was. These religious leaders were sure of what they knew, and Jesus did not fit their code of "righteousness." The problem of religiosity around the world is centered in their limitation of the knowledge of the Lord. The prophet Hosea declared that the people of God perish for lack of knowledge (Hos. 4:6).

THE PROBLEM WITH PEOPLE LIES IN WHAT THEY DON'T KNOW

Ignorance is the only thing in the world that can bring destruction to the psyche of believers. Anything that is messed up in your life by the enemy has been given entrance by ignorance of the power and the love of God. The greatest force that can destroy the people of God is not even Satan; God does not give him so much credibility. But ignorance, the prophet declared, will destroy them. As soon as the people of God came to know the ways of the Lord, they will see a manifestation of the power of God in their lives.

The wisest man on earth declared: "A wise man is strong; yea, a man of knowledge increaseth strength" (Pr. 24:5). According to the scriptures, the source of power and strength is understanding and knowledge. There is no need to pray for power; you receive real strength and power in this Kingdom through revelation and knowledge of what Christ has provided. Jesus revealed to His disciples that all power had been given to Him on the earth. In the strength of that knowledge, they were to obey His word to go and fulfill the Great Commission.

Even during the final instructions Jesus gave to His disciples, when He told them to return to Jerusalem until they received the promise of the Father, He simply instructed them to wait. They were not there to pray for power. The promise was that the power would come after the Holy Ghost was poured out, which could not happen initially until the Day of Pentecost in the timing of God. Now that Pentecost has come, believers do not even have to wait for the promise. They can receive the power of the Holy Spirit when they enter into the revelation of that promise.

SEEKING FIRST THE KINGDOM

Again, we are confronted with the priority of seeking first the Kingdom. Instead of praying for power or for revival to come, we need to seek to know God. Then we will walk in His power and will bring revival to the earth. We will do revival. Jesus came to earth to reveal the Father, to demonstrate the Kingdom of God. He knew that the problem of mankind was not that they lacked power, but that they did not know the Source of power. They needed to be brought back into relationship with God. There they would find that all their problems would be solved.

Jesus left His power on the earth so that we could fulfill the original assignment of mankind, to take dominion over the earth and fill the earth with His glory. And He clearly revealed the fact that His followers had been given supernatural power to fulfill that assignment:

> Behold, I give unto you power to tread on serpents and scorpions, and over all the power of the enemy: and nothing shall by any means hurt you.
> **—LUKE 10:19**

The Greek word, behold means to see, not with your eyes, but with your understanding. It is similar to Jesus' explanation to the Pharisees, when He said "that ye may know" (Matt.9:6). He was

211

earnestly giving them revelation knowledge of the power that He had brought to earth and was giving to men and women who believed in Him. "Behold"—be aware, understand, realize—what I am giving to you so that you can use my power to overcome the evil in the world and establish the Kingdom of righteousness, peace, and joy.

The apostle Paul prayed for believers to receive this revelation of Christ so that they could walk in the divine power that was at their disposal:

> cease not to give thanks for you, making mention of you in my prayers; that the God of our Lord Jesus Christ, the Father of glory, may give unto you the spirit of wisdom and revelation in the knowledge of him: the eyes of your understanding being enlightened; that ye may know what is the hope of his calling, and what the riches of the glory of his inheritance in the saints, and what is the exceeding greatness of his power to us-ward who believe, according to the working of his mighty power, which he wrought in Christ, when he raised him from the dead... (emphasis mine)
> **—EPHESIANS 1:16–20**

Do you see the connection? Paul knew that the power was available. He did not ask that they receive power. He was asking that their eyes would be opened, that they would know the exceeding greatness of the divine power that Christ's death and resurrection was working in them. He echoed the cry of Jesus: "that ye might know" and "Behold". He asked that knowledge would come, that understanding would be opened so that they could walk in victory and fulfill divine destiny.

When you have revelation in your spirit, you walk in power.

You become aware of the "exceeding greatness of his power to us-ward who believe, according to the working of his mighty power" (:19). It is already working in you. Christ in you has unlimited power because it was given to Him in heaven and in earth. He is on the earth in you. What you need to operate in power is to know, to realize it is at your disposal.

When you have revelation in your spirit you walk in power.

We have limited our effectiveness through lack of knowledge. What I have called my "journey into God" took the limitations off my mind and spirit and allowed me to view the world as God does: potential territory for establishing His Kingdom principles among all people. Believing His Word becomes as natural as breathing when our eyes are opened through revelation to His greatness and His purpose for our lives as believers. Divine power flows in a supernaturally "natural" way through a life that is surrendered to the Lordship of Christ and who learns to walk in "the exceeding greatness of his power to us who believe, according to the working of his mighty power..." (Eph. 1:19).

The church of the Almighty God is established to bring glory to God on the earth – in every sphere of life. The assignment of the first couple created was to take dominion over the earth and to multiply the glory of God throughout the earth. They were to subdue it to the glory of God to extend the Kingdom of heaven throughout the earth. That is still our assignment today.

Consider seriously why you are serving the Lord. Why do you go to church? It should be to take a journey into God and to know Him. If that is the case, that knowledge will make you strong— in your career, your business, your family, and your influence in society, to bring forth restoration to your land and do exploits to the glory of the Lord. That is why you are called. He trusted you. You are the salt and light of the world, called to take dominion over your "promised land" by walking in the divine power of the Kingdom.

KINGDOM PRAYER

Please pray this prayer with me if you desire to receive divine revelation of the mighty power of God that is working within you:

> Father, open my eyes to see the exceeding greatness of your power in me that I might know You and do exploits in your name. Don't let me be satisfied with just being fruitful; I want to multiply your glory and subdue my "promised land" to your Kingdom purposes.
>
> Now, in Jesus name, I pronounce upon you the strength of the Lord that is available for those who know the Lord. I release the realization of His power and the understanding to do exploits. To have the eyes of your understanding opened to His divine purpose for your life, to understand and be strong. Let the Holy Spirit bring divine revelation to you now, that you might walk in His divine power, not allowing it to lie dormant within you, but that you might exercise His power in every area of your life, now, in the name of Jesus Christ, our wonderful Lord. Amen.

KINGDOM PRINCIPLES
FROM CHAPTER 6

---

1. God established the church on the earth as the vehicle to extend His Kingdom in the world, multiplying the number of Kingdom citizens who will fill the earth with His glory.
2. Christ will have a glorious church that is holy and without blemish. It will be a people who are surrendered totally to extending His Kingdom throughout the earth.
3. In the midst of the overwhelming darkness, God is raising up a people who will believe God and His Word and walk in His power and authority.
4. The power of God is not to lie dormant in you. It is not for "decoration" of you as a person. Nor is it to exalt you as if you were the source of the success it gives you in life.
5. The power the Lord has given us is to be used to perplex and beat down principalities and powers that have had dominion all over the earth. We are to establish the dominion of righteousness, peace, and joy in the Holy Ghost.
6. To operate in the power of God it is not prayer that you need; you need faith in the Word of God: "And Jesus came and spake unto them, saying, All power is given unto me in heaven and in earth. (Mat. 28:18)

7. The key to receiving an answer to prayer lies in the spiritual revelation you have of the ways of God.

8. When you have revelation in your spirit, you walk in power. You become aware of the "exceeding greatness of his power to us who believe, according to the working of his mighty power" (Eph. 1:19).

9. Believing His Word becomes as natural as breathing when our eyes are opened through revelation to His greatness and His purpose for our lives as believers.

10. The assignment of the first couple created was to take dominion over the earth and to multiply the glory of God throughout the earth. That is still our assignment today.

Chapter 7

PROMOTION AND EXPANSION OF THE KINGDOM

And from the days of John the Baptist until now the kingdom of heaven suffereth violence and the violent take it by force.

—MATTHEW 11:12

The mandate of the church is to promote Kingdom expansion on the earth. So, it is vital that as believers we grasp the proper relationship of the Church to Christ and to His Kingdom, as I explained earlier. Otherwise, the church becomes a mere caricature of what Christ intended and suffers irrelevance to the Kingdom of God, to believers, and to the divine purpose for which it was conceived.

As I have read the gospel accounts of the mission of Jesus as well as the Acts of the apostles, I have come to believe that the heartbeat of God is not just for us to build a great ministry for him, no matter how large and influential it may become. An ecclesiastical body such as the Roman Catholic Church can dominate cultures and governments for centuries, govern tremendous wealth of properties, etc., and yet not fulfill the Great Commission.

There are other internationally impacting protestant denominations, which were spawned during times of great revival and ingathering of souls, but have since lost their influence among unbelievers and believers alike. They became ingrown, characterized by internal power struggles, "corporate" ladder-climbing among the clergy, and arguments over their religious traditions. As a result, they have failed to be relevant to present-day culture.

The compassion of Christ for the lost has not changed. His mandate for all believers to go into the world and preach the gospel has not changed. It is the self-seeking, success-pursuing minds of religious leaders that deviate from the simplicity of the gospel of the Kingdom, leading their parishioners astray from the Biblical definition of "church".

The compassion of Christ for the lost has not changed.

Admittedly, churches are established with a variety of visions regarding the calling of God for their congregation. With that vision and calling comes a special grace to help them successfully fulfill their God-given mandate. There are churches called to be a local church serving individuals in their community. There are churches called to wield a godly influence over the life of an entire city. Other churches are called to have a nation-wide impact. And there are churches called and equipped to raise up leaders and help establish churches that will impact entire nations.

A LARGER VISION

There came a time when I discovered that my goal of being a great pastor was not enough. Pastoring the great church God had established was not the full extent of His calling for my life. When I experienced this deep dissatisfaction, I set my heart to take another journey into God. I determined to seek Him until He would speak to me about my personal mandate. When He did, I discovered a much larger vision than I ever dreamed possible.

What I learned at the end of that adventure was that God was not expecting me to pastor a local church, but to accept His calling to be a deliverer of a nation. I was not used to hearing people talk like that so when that realization came to me, it was a little frightening.

I began to understand in that divine encounter, that the great church He had given me was the instrument that He had ordained to raise up believers and powerful leaders who would take the Kingdom outside the walls of the church building and help to bring about the redemption of our nation. I began to view my pulpit as a platform to address, not only the local church, but the entire nation as my parish. That meant every member of our church had to find ways to be relevant to every aspect of society. They had to learn to do as Jesus did and eat with sinners, seek the lost, and bring redemption to them.

When the Kingdom leaves the church, the church stops living for herself. The eyes of the church are opened to the fact that we are not just attending services to have fellowship and worship God corporately. We are here because we are needed by God to be co-laborers with Him, to be equipped to receive His assignments and become His hands to restore the peoples of earth back to Himself.

NOTHING WRONG WITH THE HARVEST

Then Jesus went about all the cities and villages, teaching in their synagogues, preaching the gospel of the kingdom, and healing every sickness and every disease among the people. But when He saw the multitudes, He was moved with compassion for them, because they were weary and scattered, like sheep having no shepherd. Then He said to His disciples, 'The harvest truly is plentiful, but the laborers are few. Therefore pray the Lord of the harvest to send out laborers into His harvest.

—MATTHEW 9:35-38

What is happening here? Jesus was going about the city one day and He saw a crowd of people, much like you would see in any large city. But Matthew's observation was that Jesus was moved with compassion for these people. In some way, Jesus showed His loving concern for their weariness, their lost-ness. His disciples witnessed Jesus' compassion for these "sheep having no shepherd."

First of all, it is interesting to note that Jesus in other places refers to unbelievers as "goats" and to believers as "sheep" (Matt. 25:32-33). But Jesus was looking at this multitude of unsaved people and understood they were not goats in God's perspective. They were potential sheep. He was not faulting them for being lost. They were scattered sheep who needed a shepherd. He does not say they were scattered because they were sinners, but because they had no shepherd to guard them and care for them.

Jesus was trying to get His disciples to understand their responsibility for the harvest. The harvest is synonymous with our modern term, "revival", as it refers to an ingathering of souls. He was explaining that the problem does not lie with a lack of revival—there is nothing wrong with the harvest; it is plentiful. But the laborers—the shepherds—are few.

As I mentioned earlier, simply praying for revival is not the answer to the harvest. I tell my church that it is ignorance to pray for revival—revival is plenteous. So how do you pray? You need to pray for people who are supposed to be shepherds and laborers to have their eyes opened to their primary assignments. Pray for yourself to have revelation of the Kingdom priority. Pray for freedom from distraction, including the focus on "church-work", so that you can lift up your eyes to see the "revival"—the harvest of souls that is plenteous.

William Booth, founder of the now worldwide Salvation Army organization, declared, "We must wake ourselves up! Or somebody else will take our place, and bear our cross, and thereby rob us of our crown". He was filled with righteous passion to reach the downtrodden with the gospel message by going to where they lived in their blindness and moral depravity. Born in Nottingham, England in 1829, he was sent to work in a pawnbroker's shop at the age of 13 to help support his mother and sisters. He did not enjoy his job but it made him keenly aware of the poverty in which people lived and the humiliation and degradation they suffered because of it. As a teenager he was born-again and immediately spent much of his spare time trying to persuade other people to become Christians too.

As an adult, he became a Methodist minister, travelling around preaching and sharing God's word to all who would listen. But he did not feel he had found his destiny. In 1865 he resigned his position as a Methodist minister and began preaching to the poorest of the poor in the streets of the East End of London. Some ministers who heard him preaching were so impressed that they asked him to lead a series of meetings they were holding in a large tent. As he preached to the poor and wretched there, he soon realized he had found his destiny.

Booth soon formed his own movement, which he called The Christian Mission. For years, he preached in these English "ghettos", suffering wounds from rocks thrown at him, and becoming discouraged with the results. Then, in 1878, he changed the name of his mission to The Salvation Army.

The idea of an Army fighting sin caught the imagination of the people and the Army began to grow rapidly. Booth's fiery sermons and sharp imagery drove the message home and more and more people were converted to become a soldier in the Salvation Army, accepting their destiny to bring others to Christ. By the time Booth was promoted to Glory in 1912 the Army was at work in 58 countries.

William Booth was consumed with the destiny God had given him, declaring, "While women weep, as they do now, I'll fight; while children go hungry, as they do now, I'll fight; while men go to prison, in and out, in and out, as they do now, I'll fight; while there is a drunkard left, while there is a poor lost girl upon the streets, while there remains one dark soul without the light of God, I'll fight, I'll fight to the very end!

There is nothing wrong with the harvest.

God began to give me understanding that every member of the church is a shepherd. The apostle Paul clearly teaches the importance of the five key equipping gifts of the church for equipping believers. And a pastor gifted as an equipping five fold pastor is to view the members of his or her church as pastors to the city—to the multitude who are scattered without shepherds. You send these shepherds out of the church into every aspect of society to meet these scattered sheep. According to our religious mindset we think that the place of the shepherd is in the church building. But Jesus pointed the disciples to the scattered sheep as he viewed them milling about the city without a shepherd.

The sheep are supposed to be in the field. And the shepherd is supposed to be with them in the field. God made me understand that you will never get the whole city to come to your church. The place where the city is supposed to be pastored is in the "field" where the sheep are living and working. That is God's agenda: for the Kingdom to leave the church. The people who come to the church are supposed to be trained to be on-site shepherds in the community, city, or nation to pastor the people that God has sent them to pastor.

Every member of the church is a shepherd.

So the sheep are scattered because the people who are supposed to shepherd them are not aware of their responsibility as believers. They are Christians who come to church to do God's service. While there is a legitimate service to the house of God, it should not be at the expense of your labor in the harvest field. He needs your service to bring in the harvest, to care for the lost sheep out there.

The reason you come to church on Sundays is to get trained for your ministry outside of the church, where you are a pastor—a God-carrier. The Kingdom of God is within you, the Redeemer is within you, and must find your place of service to reach the lost sheep He loves. That is His heartbeat, His great compassion, which He wants to reveal through you so that His glory can fill the earth through multiplied redemption.

I believe Jesus did not call the multitude "goats" because He understood their plight. They were simply lost sheep. As soon

223

as you see people as unbelievers, you erect a wall so that you will not be contaminated. You have the mentality that you are the Christian, and they are all unsaved people. That sense of superiority raises an invisible wall between the church and the world. It makes Christians feel like an elite society of believers who are not like others. You need to look at unsaved people as your lost brothers and sisters, potential believers, pastors, and God-carriers.

Potentially all lost sheep can be saved because Jesus has paid the price for their salvation. We ought not look at anyone as outside of the grace of God to reach them. They cannot be saved without receiving Him as Lord and Savior; they have to be born again. And they cannot be born again as long as they are scattered, with no shepherd. To be a shepherd does not mean to be a preacher. It means to care for the needs of people and guide them into green pastures, love them and let the love of Jesus draw them to Himself.

WHAT IS EVANGELISM?

In my church, we don't do typical church type evangelism. I teach my church that everyone is to seek God for their "promised land"—not just a good paying job—which is where they are called and equipped to present the gospel message. Their goal is to be God-carriers and they understand that their place of employment is a platform for sharing the love of Jesus Christ and extending the principles of the Kingdom. Salary is not the only compensation for their labor. They are not "employees"; they are primarily agents of God, His servants, Kingdom-carriers. They are here to live the lifestyle of the Kingdom. That is what it means to seek first the Kingdom, to seek its advancement throughout the earth. That is the meaning of life as a believer.

Because, when they leave the church, the Kingdom of God leaves the church, these believers are motivated with the priority of spreading the Kingdom to every sphere of life where they find themselves. They see the pastoring of lost sheep as their prime objective in life. That is the primary reason why 2 million people have come with them to church during that first years to get saved. They came with their "pastor"—the shepherd who demonstrated loving care for their soul.

When pastors ask me how we are doing evangelism to have such a growing congregation, I share this "evangelism plan" with them. It is simply training your people to lift up their eyes and see that there is nothing wrong with the harvest. It involves teaching them that they are called to be laborers with God. That is the Biblical strategy for evangelism.

Thankfully, our problem is not that no one has been saved in our church for a year. Our problem is what to do with the harvest that is so plentiful that our "nets are breaking." That wonderful "problem" is a result of teaching believers to take the Kingdom outside of the church and to have the right mindset about their calling and priority.

All of our people are trained to see themselves as a shepherd or pastor in the field where they live and work. They come to church to pray for the "territory" for which they are responsible. They fast one or two days a week for the people they are supposed to be caring for. The reason they study in the Bible School or take other university studies is to improve certain skills, to be able to communicate the gospel better to the people for whom they are responsible.

With this perspective, church makes sense. Church members do not attend church for 10 years and become bored or contentious, deciding to look for a "better" church. Believers who connect with God's heartbeat for the lost will become established in the church. They will humbly seek God for empowerment to be an effective God-carrier in their sphere of influence. People who do not make the spreading of the Kingdom their priority just come to church week after week, doing the same thing, which is suffocating, robbing them of life. That is why people run from one church to another.

I tell my church that my assignment as their pastor is "to get rid of you." To get you out of the pews—that is my assignment. No one has a calling to sit in the pews of a church. The only calling we have is to "Go." And that calling is for everyone. So when the Kingdom leaves the church, having been properly equipped, there is potential for mass salvations in your community, city or nation.

No one has a calling to sit in the pews of a church.

Because of the phenomenal growth of our church in our city, I have been accused of using black magic to bring people into the church. The influence of our members in every sphere of society is so effective, people think we have millions of church members instead of thousands. The fact is that though many people have received salvation through our church and these, in turn, have influenced other people. Over 250,000 people report that they have been touched by our church because they came and received salvation and are involved in the church in some way. We recognize 100,000 active members all over the country. We refer to our church as a church without walls. Every member of the church is training to become a faithful laborer in the harvest. That is revival, and it is spreading throughout our city, our nation, and into other nations of the world.

SEVEN SPHERES OF INFLUENCE

There has to be a specific strategy developed for being effective in reaping the harvest. Changing the metaphor, in order for the Kingdom to leave the church, believers need to know how to become shepherds. So I began to teach our people to discover their promised land in relation to the seven major spheres of influence, according to sociologists, which I listed earlier. These main categories of life pursuits include business and economics, arts and culture, sports, social/spiritual pursuits, education, entertainment and media, and the political arena.

My goal was to help them to identify where they are personally destined to function as a Kingdom builder where they live their lives—outside the church. Without that understanding, they may wander around in the general "category" of their calling, but live in confusion and frustration without finding their specific "niche." For example, those who are equipped by God to function in social or spiritual pursuits may tend to   want to be pastors of a church. That desire can be misguided because leaders in the church have emphasized the idea that greatness in the Kingdom means to become a great pastor or teacher.

But when people who desire to function in the social/spiritual sphere understand that it is much broader than serving a church as a pastor, they begin to explore the full calling they have been given. Teaching in an inner city high school can have a much greater impact on young lives than preaching a sermon behind the pulpit of a church, for example.

Sharing the love of Jesus to hurting, desperate youth and giving them hope of finding fulfillment in life is taking territory for the King, restoring the Kingdom of God to the earth. Unwed mothers, alcoholics, drug addicts, divorcees, veterans, the poor, and many other lost and hurting elements of society are calling for anointed God-carriers. They need to experience the love of a Kingdom person to care for them and restore them to their Savior.

In our church in Kyiv, we have taught the people that where ever they have a burden, that could be their ministry. Therefore we encourage them to start their own social organizations (NGOs - non-governmental organizations or NPOs – non profit organizations). Sometimes these are apart from their jobs, or professions. Through these organizations they can be involved in the outreach they are destined to fulfill.

Today we have members of our church involved in such organizations, addressing almost every problem in society. The fact is that the church is supposed to be concerned with every challenge, or ill of the society. We are supposed to be the salt of the earth, so through our church, in all of the aforementioned categories of distinct spheres of society, we are helping to bring people to Christ and resolving their problems. These organizations were not started by the church, but actually by individual members who have a burden for that particular area of life.

The organizations belong to the individual believers, not to the local churches. Of course our individual believers still recognize and honor the spiritual leadership of the pastor and leaders of their local churches. Thus, people who have a burden for unwed mothers, divorcees, etc. go out and start organizations to reach out to them. Others might have a burden for war veterans or for the poor or another need represented by a segment of society. What ever organization they start becomes a platform for them to minister the gospel to that group of people.

Spiritual/Social sphere

The spiritual sphere of life is linked with the social sphere, according to sociology. But I want to address the spiritual arena separately for a moment, because it causes so many believers confusion when seeking to discover their promised land. When church leaders emphasize only "classical" ministry positions in a church as a potential territory for serving God, people who are not called to pastor a church can become frustrated. They feel a desire to help meet social and spiritual needs but are not called to classical ministry. They may try to compete with the pastor and create a split in the church instead of finding their "promised land" of social or spiritual service where they have been called to be effective, fruitful, and fulfilled.

When I began to teach this principle of finding your personal destiny, people began to realize that they are not all called to be pastors or pulpit ministers. They understood that every member could actually be fulfilled without necessarily fighting for the "pulpit", which could result in splitting the church. They are free to fulfill their destiny because the pastor encourages them to go and fulfill their personal destiny and calling.

The next question that people ask is, "What happens to those who are called as pastors and pulpit ministers?" Well, as soon as I or they recognize that they have this calling, they go through a training process in the church to prepare them to become pastors. Then they are encouraged to step out of our church and launch their own ministries. As their pastor, besides giving these new pastors members from the central church to help them establish their new congregation, I also finance their churches for at least one year to help them get established.

When aspiring pastors and ministers see this kind of support, there is basically no desire to split our church because they know they are being helped to come into their own destiny as pastors. As a result, we have established 35 churches just in the city of Kyiv, all of which have different registered names, identities, offices and bookkeeping entities. This standard of helping pastors get established largely explains why church splits are not a problem for our church in Kyiv.

That is my agenda as an equipping pastor: to get rid of my parishioners. So, you want to be a pastor like me? Let me help you. I sponsor you for a year in your own territory and help you become the pastor you are called to become. In that way we have been able to establish over 700 churches in the last 10 years.

My agenda as a pastor is to get rid of my members, moving them from the pews into society.

Helping the Poor / Social sphere

There are those who are called specifically to minister to the needy. Their hearts are moved with compassion when they see hurting people in many aspects of society's ills. The homeless, orphans, women's issues of abortion and domestic violence, single mothers, prisoners, young people without fathers, and as many other social issues as you can think of are crying out for God-carriers to bring the Kingdom of heaven to them.

I ask our people to present to our leadership the area of need for which they feel a burden. Then I tell them that we will form a platform by which to reach that troubled segment of humanity. I don't encourage them as an individual just to try to minister to addicts, for example. Instead, we look for others with that same burden and form a team to establish a Drug Rehabilitation Center.

We have established over 3,000 social organizations, of which 600 are registered with the government in our nation. Individuals who have the proper training for the field of social service in which they are involved establish these. Our church is an umbrella for over 600 officially registered social organizations meeting the needs of many different aspects of society's hurting people.

Each organization has its own leadership and a team of people working with them. They are not registered as a "church" because local churches have a different role and purpose. Their role is to become a voice for wholeness in a specific sphere of society, teaching the principles of the Kingdom. For example, marriage counselors teach young couples how to establish a strong home based on Christian principles. Drug rehabilitation Centers help young people turn away from their addictions and lead productive lives. They are so effective that the government listens to them; the social groups listen to them. The unions listen to them. They are functioning everywhere. We have several hundred Rehabilitation Centers and over 50 homes for street children alone registered with the government (NGOs or NPOs).

Political Arena for this Section

In our nation, it is not unusual to have many different political parties championing their own specific agenda. If you feel a calling to persuade people in the political arena toward Christian policies, I encourage you to join an existing political party or to form your own. Carefully planned with articulated political agendas, there are three political parties that have come out of our church. And other members have joined existing parties to champion Christian values in the city and nation.

In our last city election for Kiev, there were 48 candidates running to become mayor of the city of 4 million people. Two of the candidates were from our church and one of them was elected mayor of Kiev. This man did not consider himself to be a classical politician. He saw himself as a businessman. But when I began to teach regarding the seven spheres of society, I explained that one way to recognize your calling is to consider what is annoying you.

Whatever ill of society you see that irritates you indicates that you have a burden for that area of need. It matters to you. It may seem that others are not doing it right or are not doing enough.

You have ideas of how to make it work, how to make it better. I tell my people not to whine or complain about what you see; do something about it. That is your burden for extending the Kingdom in that sphere of life.

This businessman recognized that he had a burden for city government and understood ways that they could do things better for the good of the people. It grieved him to hear of corruption and injustice when it seemed so unnecessary to him. Because of my influence he began to understand his calling to civic leadership and God opened the doors for him to be elected Mayor of Kiev. His party controls 30% of the city Parliament.

Because of this understanding, during the last election we had several hundred members of our church running for political office. They had established teams through the years to gain positions of influence in the political arena where their goal is to extend the principles of the Kingdom in civic and social arenas through the political platform. Many in our congregatons are making a difference in the political sphere as they accept the challenge to bring Kingdom values, principles, and lifestyle to our government.

Educational Sphere

Tetiana Galushka is a member of our church who dropped out of school in the seventh grade, got pregnant, became a drug addict and a prostitute. She came to our church and received Christ as her Savior. But her self-esteem was battered and she felt she would never become a person of value. As she continued attending services for six years, she began to believe in the transformation that God was working in her life. She decided to go back to school and take evening classes to graduate with her daughter.

Then she enrolled in a university for the purpose of training so that she could help prevent young people from taking the path to immorality that she had taken. She has authored a brilliant curriculum for that purpose, which has been adopted by the Department of Education of Ukraine

Other members have written special curricula for high schools on ethics and moral living. Because there was not previously presented programs like these, the Department of Education of Ukraine has adopted them to be taught in the high schools of our nation. These are the kinds of things that can happen when the Kingdom leaves the pews of the church.

Men's ministries have also flourished in our church as we realized that no one is teaching boys how to become men, husbands, and fathers. We began to consider how many of the problems of our society were connected to this lack of understanding of manhood. There are curricula for teaching professions like professors and physicians, but few classes to teach youth to be a real man. And there are few role models who exemplify Christian values in these areas.

The same dilemma faces young women regarding how to become a wife and mother and the proper way to raise children. Without spiritual guidance, girls become pawns for sexual pleasure and never really understand how to establish a marriage or home that will last.

People who have a burden for these needs in our church came together and formed the Institute of Family and Fatherhood. They wrote curricula addressing issues from dating to marriage, to pregnancy, to being a successful father and mother. That program was presented to the government and they were so impressed that they now sponsor the entire Institute and pay all our workers as well.

Business and Economics

One of the members of our church was a successful business woman. She heard me teach that the purpose of business is not just to make a lot of money and bring tithes and offerings to church. I taught that such a mindset represented much too small a vision or purpose. I explained that the main purpose of business is to bring the principles of God's Kingdom into a particular sphere of business and extend His reign. The primary mission of a business person is to bring the influence of God to that area of business.

I teach business professionals how to strategize and release the power of the prosperity of the Kingdom through their business. I established schools to teach these strategies so that people who are called to business don't just sell their products; they are involved in communicating the principles of the Kingdom through their business.

The fact that you earn money from your business simply means that God gave you the opportunity and talent to serve Him in the arena of business. Have you considered that one of your roles is to partner with others who are doing a service for the King? Have you considered that this ministry or service may need funds which can be generated from marketplace activities? When you pay tithes from your business, you are fulfilling a Biblical obedience in surrendering to His will (Mal. 3:10). Offerings are also a Biblical way to serve God with finances. But you understand that all the money belongs to Him; He has simply made you the manager and steward of your finances.

A business woman from my church heard my message and allowed it to impact her own life. She had been an alcoholic herself for thirty years and felt she would never be free or live a life of worth. As she listened to the Word, she was delivered from alcoholism and began to form a team of former alcoholics and drug addicts to minister to needy people. They established a Rehabilitation Center in our church and to date, there have been 10,000 people in our church who have been delivered from drugs and alcohol through their ministry.

They have trained other teams to establish Rehabilitation Centers and at present there are over 600 centers across our nation helping people be set free through the power of the gospel. Remember, the goal is not to just reap a small harvest in one church or city, but to reclaim the entire Promised Land —little by little. As you train those who have been delivered, the vision is to reclaim all of society from drug abuse and alcoholism.

A very unique business outreach that we have established is called Club 1000. The goal of Club 1000 is to develop 1000 millionaires in five years. These are not to be simply successful businessmen and women, but Christians with high moral standards and Kingdom values, and a focus on extending the Kingdom. Aimed at the financial development of each of its members, it conducts numerous purposeful training seminars that address issues involved in the deliberate, habitual development of wealth leading to becoming a millionaire.

With several hundred members, the club holds regular sessions and meetings which have resulted in establishing trust and forming strong networks between the members for the realization and success of high income projects. As the result of effective cooperation of these business-teams, they have organized models of economic development in real estate, construction, internet-technologies, stock-exchange activities, consulting, wedding agencies, tourism, and health activities. Committees have been formed to facilitate these pursuits, including land, banking, business-projects committees, and others.

Members of Club 1000 take an active civil role in many social projects as well, including the Social Organization for

"Mothers of Ukraine", The International Mission for "Revival of Nations", etc. They are welcoming new Associates who want to make an impact on society through the world of finance. (For more information about the business sphere and club 1000, read my book Money Won't Make You Rich (Lake Mary, FL: Charisma House, A Strang Company, 2008)

Sports Arena

Perhaps the sports arena seems irrelevant to some for extending the Kingdom of God because it represents only recreation and fun. Yet, stadiums are overflowing with hundreds of thousands of "fans" around the world who enjoy watching their teams or individual athletes compete in every imaginable kind of sport. It seems logical that God is interested in redeeming these "fans" for His purposes. He is looking for born-again believers who will be God-carriers in the arena of sports venues.

Morgan Shepherd has been driving in the American NASCAR Sprint Cup series of races for over 20 years. He has not been a big winner, but his main focus is not on winning the race but on winning souls. An article was published called "Good Shepherd: Driver Focused More on Winning Souls than Races" tells his story.

"When he travels to the racetrack every weekend, he has two jobs. The first is to get his Faith Motorsports entry into the starting lineup and finish as high up in the standings as possible. But the second job – and the one he places the most emphasis on – is using his Victory in Jesus Racing ministry to spread his faith in Jesus to as many people as possible. Anyone who's heard Shepherd share his testimony knows he's not afraid to tell it like it is, and he makes no bones about the fact that there are a lot of souls out there for the taking among the ranks of NASCAR fans.

Recently, he has moved higher up in the standings, and he says he likes to think his recent success will only serve to increase his ability to serve God. "I've seen such a good opportunity being in the sport – it's my mission field – to encourage people to better their lives, and doing that by carrying the Jesus logo on the hood of the car we've been able to reach people all over the world. I was just amazed to get fan mail from Russia, Germany, Australia and all over the world saying they appreciate our stand in racing. I like to think that Jesus logo on the hood gets people to thinking," he said.

One viewer from Africa who saw Shepherd on TV talking about a young man named Josh Hill, who was hit by a drunk driver was himself an alcoholic. This was one of the afflictions that plagued Shepherd's life before he was saved. "This guy heard me tell about it, and then when I prayed he received Christ. He sent us an e-mail, and he even sent one to the church I go to. All the way from Africa he sought us out and encouraged us with what a difference it had made in his life. We know we're doing something to point people in the right direction, and I've got many many stories like that – what's happened to people by us being there."

Athletes who find their platform for sharing the love of Jesus in a sports arena can become role models for young and old alike and wield great influence for bringing them to Christ. Another powerful example of a life-long witness to the Kingdom reality in this arena is the American football coach, Tony Dungy. For 30 years, he has been an admired and highly successful football player and then head coach in the National Football League (NFL).

Upon Tony's recent announcement of retirement, his peers in that arena, television commentators and analysts of the game of football, asked each other if they had ever heard Tony Dungy say a negative word about anyone or lose his temper. Their answers were all the same; they had only heard Tony speaking softly and in an encouraging tone to everyone, including his team. This is more remarkable in an arena where "macho" strength is usually demonstrated with screaming marked by profanity to correct the mistakes that were made during a game.

Tony's goal was to change the culture of professional football, by bringing the Kingdom principles of respect and decency in all his dealings with players and other personnel in the NFL. Through his godly lifestyle, he demonstrated the values of the Kingdom and redefined the concept of the strength of a man's success.

Tony Dungy wrote a book titled Quiet Strength: The Principles, Practices, and Priorities of a Winning Life to express the truth about the inner strength that motivated him to succeed in the sports arena. He said that real strength comes from the inside, from knowing that God is in control and that He empowers you to exert a strong influence for righteousness in your environment, one person at a time or millions at a time. When the Baltimore Colts won the Super Bowl, Tony Dungy used the platform of the post-game celebration to speak to millions of people about his faith in Jesus Christ. His books is a #1 Best Seller and he has published a Men's Bible Study along with it as well.

Tony Dungi redefined the strength of a man's success.

Tony's motivation was not simply to win championships with his football team, which he did accomplish. He said, "I really wanted to show people you can win all kinds of ways...for your faith to be more important than your job...we all know that's the way it should be...I'm not afraid to say it."

Christian athletes have a unique opportunity to become role models, not only for excellence in their sport, but for the way they live their lives to extend Kingdom principles and influence those who appreciate their success. Their fan base as well as fellow athletes can become their promised land, where they can sow seeds of truth and life and reap a great harvest of souls.

Arts and Culture

There are some who would concede the arts arena to the devil. They are convinced that people really want to listen to vile lyrics and lewd songs, that they are determined to view lustful, forbidden scenes for pleasure. Yet, as in every other arena, many people are making choices based on what is popular and "cool." When Christian leaders dare to invade, with authority, the devil's domain with the uplifting, hopeful, and redemptive ideas and attitudes of the Kingdom, people listen.

A group of young people in our church were looking for a way to influence other young people, so they decided to look for an area that would be of interest to youth. They developed a game, much like the board game, Monopoly. They called it, "University of Life Games". The game is played so that if you follow the wrong set of life principles, you go to prison, get hooked on drugs, or even go to hell. On the other hand, if you follow the correct (Kingdom) set of principles, this will lead to your health, prosperity, and eternal life! Through this game, a lot of young people have discovered the truth about peace with God and living a Christian life.

"University of Life Games" addresses issues of developing your abilities and talents, making friends, becoming a leader and even learning the possibilities of financial development. It helps young people believe in themselves and develop their personalities to influence the world. The goal is to help the youth to find their goals and dreams—and fulfill them! So successful has been the game, "University of Life Games", that is now a Ukraine-wide youth movement, having gathered more than 5,000 young people who have played the game and bought it. "University of Life Games" has opened doors for young people in 12 countries.

The game is played at corporate training sessions, business parties and home parties, and many other small group situations. It is a training program based on modern methods of developing practical skills in effective communication, management, team building, public speaking, and practical business undertakings.

The "University of Life" credit union is a ministry and training in stable financial structures. It proclaims the values of God's Kingdom regarding financial markets and serves people who want training in finance and starting small businesses.

Another success story involving the arts involves Sergiy, a former casino owner who received Christ and wanted to discover his promised land to redeem it for the Kingdom. He was interested in the arts and decided to produce a movie that would illustrate the principles of the Kingdom, especially for youth. His first film, titled "One for All", was fast paced and funny, yet demonstrated the serious principles of Jesus giving His life for all of humanity. This movie became the most popular youth film for 2005, attracting a fan club of over 12 million people.

There is no territory on earth that cannot be redeemed and restored to the King. When believers truly accept the challenge to discover their promised land, they will be surprised at the influence they can have against the encroachment of the evil one on the minds and hearts of "lost sheep." As co-laborers with Christ, we have all the resources of heaven at our disposal. He conquered the forces of darkness on the cross; it is our assignment to enforce the victory of Calvary and turn the minds of people from darkness to that wonderful light. No assignment is too difficult; just as leaven does its silent, invisible work, so are we to be on the earth as agents of redemption.

Media and Entertainment

Closely related to the Arts and Culture, the media and entertainment sphere is just as controversial for many Christians. Unbelievers who often mock religion dominate it; some even engage in blasphemous tirades against a God they do not believe exists. Believers should shun this form of entertainment. But that does not mean that believers should exclude themselves from invading this arena to use this platform for reclaiming territory for the Kingdom of God.

For example, beauty pageants have become a platform for some beautiful Christian young ladies to share their philosophy of life and use their influence to win others to the message of the Kingdom.

Lika, a beautiful young lady, had attended our church since she was 8 years old. As she matured, she began to understand that it was God who had given her the beauty that people attributed to her. She realized that she could make it a platform for giving her testimony and using her influence to share the principles of the Kingdom.

So, she entered the national beauty pageant at the last minute and God gave her favor to become the reigning Miss Ukraine 2007. She has used her national exposure to be a lovely spokesperson in various media outlets, sharing freely the principles of the Kingdom of love.

THE INCREASE OF THE KINGDOM OF GOD

Of the increase of His government and peace there will be no end, upon the throne of David and over His kingdom, to order it and establish it with judgment and justice from that time forward, even forever. The zeal of the Lord of hosts will perform this.

—ISAIAH 9:7

As you seek to know God and His destiny for your life, you will enter into an exciting adventure of finding your "promised land." And you will begin to walk in His divine power to extend the Kingdom throughout the earth. God prophesied His passion for restoration of His Kingdom through Isaiah. He saw into the heart, the pain, the burden of God for the future of the world.

God said things are not going to continue as they have always been with Satan walking the earth and ruling indiscriminately, bringing destruction to God's creation. There is a time coming when God shall arise in His glory and his enemies shall be scattered. That time would be signified when He sent His son (Isa. 9:6) and because of that event a new day would be restored to the earth. The Kingdom glory that was lost on the face of the earth was going to begin to be restored.

From the time Jesus came and began to preach the Kingdom of heaven, His divine government would progressively grow and increase, and that increase would know no end. Through His death and resurrection at Calvary, that government of righteousness, peace, and joy in the Holy Ghost (Rom. 14:17) was established and it will one day rule the earth. That is the passion in the heart of God.

So Jesus brought the Kingdom and preached it during His ministry on earth. As He prepared to return to His Father, He established the citizens of the Kingdom, the church. It was intended to be a vehicle for restoring the Kingdom principles and lifestyle to the earth. The earth will only be redeemed back to its rightful owner through the good news of the Kingdom. So Jesus brought the Kingdom and He declared to us that he had brought good news, that we could be transferred into the Kingdom and extend the reign and dominion of God throughout the earth.

Jesus declared that the Kingdom of God is within us and that He would build His church and the gates of hell would not prevail against it (Matt. 16:18). His church is the instrument for what Isaiah prophesied. As believers, we are ordained to work and live for the increase of His government and dominion on the earth. He designed the church to specifically facilitate the increase of His Kingdom.

We need to realize that the Kingdom of God is within us. The Kingdom is not represented by an ecclesiastical expression of religious traditions. The church is established to equip believers to discern the Kingdom of God and extend His domain throughout the earth. The equipping ministry of the apostle, prophet, evangelist, pastor, and teacher is responsible to help believers carry the Kingdom values and lifestyle into the world with grace, proficiency, ability, wisdom and strength. In this way, the Kingdom will be extended and of the increase of His government, there will be no end. I invite you to pray with me:

KINGDOM PRAYER

Dear Lord Jesus, You are the King of Kings and the Lord of Lords. I acknowledge that your Kingdom dwells within me; that Christ in me is the hope of glory. Please help me in my journey to know You and to discover the specific strategy you have for my life. Let me be filled with the zeal of the Lord to extend your Kingdom throughout the earth in the sphere of influence to which you have called me. I determine to seek you until I hear your voice giving me direction and empowering me to believe your Word. Thank you for saving me. Help me to walk in faith in your Word to fulfill my destiny and become an effective laborer in the end-time harvest. It is in your name I pray. Amen.

KINGDOM PRINCIPLES
FROM CHAPTER 7

---

1. The mandate of the church is to promote Kingdom expansion throughout the earth.
2. When the Kingdom leaves the church, the church stops living for herself.
3. There is nothing wrong with the harvest; it will come in if the workers go out into the fields.
4. Lost sheep are scattered because the people who are supposed to shepherd them are not aware of their responsibility as believers.
5. The goal of believers is to be God-carriers into their place of employment, which is primarily a platform for sharing the love of Jesus Christ and extending the principles of the Kingdom.
6. My assignment as a pastor is "to get rid of" my parishioners, to get them out of the pews. No one has a calling to sit in the pews of a church. The only calling we have is to "Go".
7. Whatever ill of society you see that you think needs to be addressed indicates that you have a burden for that area of need. It is likely your "promised land."
8. The fact that you earn money from your business simply means that God gave you the opportunity and talent to serve

Him in the arena of business.

9. When Christian leaders dare to invade, with authority, the devil's domain with the uplifting, hopeful, and redemptive ideas and attitudes of the Kingdom, people listen.

10. The church is established to equip believers to discern the Kingdom of God and extend its dominion throughout the earth.

Chapter 8

THE PURSUIT OF THE KINGDOM

"And I bestow upon you a Kingdom, just as My Father bestowed one upon Me,"

—LUKE 22:29

Every generation must reclaim their generation for God. There is truth to the old saying that God has no grandchildren. Personal commitment to the principles of the Kingdom must take pre-eminence in the lives of every believer who wants to see his or her generation comes to know God. It is the responsibility of each new generation to restore the authority of God in government, in business, in education, in entertainment, in every sphere of life of their nation.

Throughout church history, you can point to men and women of God who took responsibility to compel their nations to adopt the values and lifestyle of the Kingdom in their nations.

The generation of Jonathan Edwards, George Finney, and other godly heroes of the American church were responsible for mighty revivals—great harvests of souls—restoring the authority of God to their generation. Oral Roberts, T. L. Osborn and others distributed the healing power of God on America and in other nations in the last generation.

Every generation must reclaim their generation back to God

The reason America has been known as a Christian nation is because of these great people, ministries and powerful revivals that impacted the culture and influenced society as a whole. America was established on Judeo-Christian values that are embedded in the Constitution and still guide the laws of the land. Their core values are based on honesty, integrity, and civil liberties. Even though liberal lawmakers and judges have seriously eroded these values more recently, the blessing of God is still evident on the land. The whole world wants to run to America to live there because of the prosperity it has achieved through Kingdom principles that insure liberty and justice for all.

In this current generation, however, the church is not prospering in its mandate to extend Kingdom principles throughout the culture, as statistics we mentioned previously show. It is our responsibility as believers to compel the adoption of the virtues and principles of the Kingdom, creating respect throughout the earth for the church. We must demonstrate the love of God in our spheres of influence—our promised land —so that people will want to come back to God to find the fulfillment and satisfaction they see in us.

A Minneapolis-based Search Institute directed a survey toward religious interests of American youth. The first question was,

"What does it mean to be spiritual?" There were nine choices, running from "believing in God" to "being true to one's inner self." They also could say that there is no spiritual dimension, and there was an "I don't know" option. A positive result of the survey (which involved 6,853 participants) is that 93 percent of the young people surveyed believe there is a spiritual aspect to life.

And 55 percent of young people ages 12 to 25 say they are more spiritual now than two years ago. But nearly one-third of the young people said they don't trust organized religion. They equate being spiritual with a sense of "harmony." And religion is equated more with dogma. The disconnect between spirituality and religion was clear in the comments from a young man named Ian who says he is highly spiritual but not at all religious.

In this context, spirituality is a vague realization of relating to a supernatural cosmos, universe, or moral standard. Religion is the product of organizations called churches. This survey is one more that reveals the lack of effectiveness the church today is having on our society.

When the authority of the church has been lifted up and made visible, the nations will come to the church, as the prophet declared. The church will have answers for the problems of society that no psychiatrist or business commission will have. The church will demonstrate real Kingdom values in the middle of economic downturn. It is the church that must teach the ways of God, to proclaim the law out of Zion and the word of the Lord from Jerusalem. For that to happen, believers in every sphere of life must be seeking God and taking His presence into society so that the people will follow them to the source of Life— to God Himself.

FAULTY MOTIVATION OF BELIEVERS

Have you paid attention to why people go to church today? It is for miracles or to seek prosperity. Because of a faulty, compromised gospel that is preached widely today, people are being taught to go to church for what they can get from God. No longer do Christians gather primarily to worship God or to be equipped to be effective in bringing in the harvest. They go for ego-centric reasons to "get their needs met." They are not going to church to learn to compel the adoption of His principles and compel their promised land to the lordship of Christ.

Instead, believers are exploiting God, worshipping themselves, and wanting what they can get from God. When ego motivates them to go to church, this makes them idol worshippers. They are not bowing to worship statues or even the stars or sun; they are idolizing themselves. If you are motivated to serve God for what you can get from Him, then you become the object of worship.

When you engage in a religious form of singing, praising and praying, but your motivation is to get what you want, you are really bowing before the idol of "self." People confuse religion with true worship. The "seeker-friendly' approach to religion, that we discussed earlier, can be ego-centric; true worship is God centered. In God-centered worship, it is the will of God that becomes the passion of the believer, no matter the personal sacrifice that may be required to realize it.

The end-time church that the prophet Micah foretold will be a worshipper of God alone. And it will become so influential, that nations will come to learn the ways of God, His principles, and to walk in His paths (Mic. 4:2). That will require an amazing transformation of the church, as we know it today.

People confuse religion with true worship

THE LAST CHRISTIAN GENERATION?

Josh McDowell, prolific author and international traveling representative for Campus Crusade for Christ, is renowned for his love for the youth of America and his untiring efforts to strengthen their faith. In His book, The Last Christian Generation, Rev. McDowell cites dire predictions regarding the Christian youth of America. Various denominational leaders have confessed to him that between sixty-nine (69%) and ninety-four (94%) percent of their young people are leaving the traditional church after high school...and very few are returning. For a large majority of youth raised in church, it is obvious that the church has become irrelevant to their goals and pursuits in life.

A ground-breaking study by George Barna, founder of the Barna Group, a renowned research and resource firm, divided professed born-again Christian youth into two categories: (1) Those who believe in Christ, but their lives don't reflect Christlikeness; and (2) Those who believe in Christ and live a Christlike life. His research showed that ninety-eight (98%) of professed born-again young people do "believe in Christ," but they do not reflect Christlike attitudes or actions!

They have not been motivated to embrace the Kingdom values, principles, and lifestyle. They do not understand their destiny to be light and salt on the earth.

In a New York Times interview, Ron Luce, founder of Teen Mania, cited the fact that only four percent (4%) of teenagers will be "Bible-believing Christians" as adults if the current trends continue. That would be a sharp decline compared with 35 percent of the current generation of baby boomers, and before that, 65 percent of the World War II generation.

The world is watching to see what the church has to offer to this troubled society. Does it offer answers for the complexities of 21st century problems? The truth is that the church of Jesus Christ has the only answers that work to dispel fear, anger, hatred, broken relationships, and every ill of society. The fact is that the church is not fulfilling its role to establish the Kingdom of God throughout the earth.

Why has the American church failed to establish its youth in the truths of the Bible? In the principles of Christian living? In pursuing the destiny and lifestyle of the Kingdom? This is because it has not understood and preached the gospel of the Kingdom. It has failed to challenge them to surrender their lives to discover their God-given purpose for living.

Earlier I explained that Jesus taught His followers to "Seek first the Kingdom of God and His righteousness" (Matt. 6:33). How many believers today interpret that to mean attending church as often as possible, giving offerings, working in church programs, and becoming a "good Christian"? This type of gospel cripples believers, limiting their pursuit of God to within the four walls of the church.

I am not minimizing the importance of being committed to gathering for worship and teaching. Let me reiterate that every believer must be accountable to and functioning with each other in a local gathering of believers as the scriptures teach. But increasing church membership is not the ultimate goal of Christians; gathering together helps us to grow in grace and be equipped to extend the Kingdom throughtout the earth. The failure of the church is a result of not equipping believers with the mindset, the faith, and the tools to extend the Kingdom of God throughtout the earth.

The love of God, which is the nature of the Kingdom, must mature within you and make you a God-carrier of His Kingdom principles and power in your every day life. The evidence that this is happening will be seen in your Kingdom lifestyle. It will be demonstrated as you prioritize your life to reach into the sphere of society to which you are called to extend the principles and values of the Kingdom.

When you are succeeding in your Kingdom mission, you will become consumed with the passion, the heartbeat of God, to extend His glory in your "promised land". That passion will empower you to change your environment, impact lives, and reap the harvest of souls God has destined for you.

REDEEMING THE POLITICAL SPHERE

Alexander, a former drug addict, came to Christ and began to seek God for His promised land. He began to discover his giftings in pastoring, and eventually launched a successful church. As he continued his journey into God, he began to have a vision for transforming the political arena. He pursued that sphere of influence, launching a government-funded training program for social and government workers. He has now trained and planted over 200 people in various government institutions, equipping them with Kingdom principles for the purpose of influencing political decisions in the government.

Their goal is to use the political positions as a platform to introduce legislation based on the principles of the Kingdom of God. They are redeeming the influential sphere of government, restoring it to reflect the government of God.

For many Christians, their vocation or place of employment still seems irrelevant to their Christian experience. They categorize their lives into separate pursuits, including work, church, family, and recreation. This faulty mindset reveals a great deception regarding the destiny of every believer. I have said that the purpose of employment is not to make money just to make a living or become wealthy. Your vocation should involve you in the destiny God has ordained for you, which is to become the carrier of His Kingdom principles. Your lifestyle should reflect your passion to extend the glory of God on the earth.

THE TRUE MEASURE OF SUCCESS

> Then the King will say to those on His right hand, 'Come, you blessed of My Father, inherit the kingdom prepared for you from the foundation of the world.
> **—MATTHEW 25:34**

When Jesus taught about the Son of Man coming in His glory with the holy angels with Him, He said that He would sit on the throne of His glory. And the nations would be gathered to Him there. Then He will separate them as a shepherd divides his sheep from his goats (Matt. 25:31–33). The amazing criteria by which Christ will judge us is whether or not we fed the hungry, gave water to the thirsty, showed hospitality to strangers, clothed the naked, and visited the sick and those in prison.

Too often the church has thought that serving humanity as Jesus described is beneath their spiritual pursuits. Many Christian leaders have considered helping the poor, for example, nothing more than a powerless "social gospel." They would rather engage in church programs, helping to create a musical worship experience for the congregation, or other admittedly worthwhile tasks centered on church members. This self-serving mentality of the church has turned many young people off and made unbelievers feel that Christians are part of just another social club that focuses on taking care of their own.

To be successful according to the criteria Christ uses to judge nations, the church must leave the four walls behind and go out. The apostle Paul declared:

> …having made known to us the mystery of His will, according to His good pleasure which He purposed in Himself, that in the dispensation of the fullness of the times He might gather together in one all things in Christ, both which are in heaven and which are on earth—in Him.
>
> **—EPHESIANS 1:9–10**

It is clear from Paul's statements that God is intent on gathering together in one all things, both in heaven and on earth, into Christ. He deals not just with individuals, but also with nations. He is a redeemer of the whole world. As co-laborers with Him, we must lift our eyes to the harvest of souls that He sees and be empowered to reap it with Him.

When God created the earth, He intended that everything that has breath would praise Him and enjoy relationship with their Creator. The psalmist declared:

> Let heaven and earth praise Him, The seas and everything that moves in them. For God will save Zion and build the cities of Judah, that they may dwell there and possess it. Also, the descendants of His servants shall inherit it, and those who love His name shall dwell in it.
>
> **—PSALM 69:34–36**

This prophetic psalm shows again that God did not separate

humanity from the environment in which they were created. All the earth is to bring praise to God. And He will save Zion—the church—and every generation who loves His name will dwell there. What a wonderful promise for those who walk with God to extend His Kingdom throughout the earth. That is how the earth will be filled with the knowledge of the glory of the LORD, as the waters cover the sea (Hab. 2:14)

All things should glorify God. To that end, the church must be involved in all the seven spheres of life, extending the virtues and principles and lifestyle of the Kingdom of God. The church that will be effective in restoring the Kingdom to this generation will need to consider these truths about each sphere of life:

1. The church must know that it's fine to be involved with social life and bring life to the community.
2. Church and business are compatible: this is the only way the riches of the wicked can come into the hands of the righteous.
3. The education system is to be integrated with the Word of God because through knowledge, wisdom and understanding is the power to bring light to the darkness.
4. God and government can work together because God Himself made government.
5. Culture and holiness must be made compatible in the environment of the Kingdom.
6. Media must not be allowed to carry only bad news; the gospel (good news) must be represented through the media.
7. Godliness should characterize sports and promote the positive worth of exercise and fitness.

Finding your personal promised land where you can thrive and be fulfilled is the ultimate destiny of every Christian. Your destiny will be fulfilled as you extend Kingdom principles and lifestyle on the earth. And the church's main task is to help believers do just that. In that sense, the church acts as a clearinghouse for believers, to give direction, guidance, and skills to help its members mature in the calling that Christ has given to each of them.

A HOUSE OF PRAYER FOR ALL NATIONS

Jesus expressed outrage in the temple the day He overturned the money changers' tables and accused them of making His Father's house a den of thieves. How outraged would He be today if He were to enter some of our churches? According to Jesus, His house is to be a house of prayer for all nations (Matt. 21:13). How different would our churches be if our priority were to seek God earnestly to show us how to extend His Kingdom —in our lives, our community, our nation, and in the nations of the world?

As I write these pages, I am consumed with the passion of the heart of God. I am concerned with what concerns Him. What is that? For the earth to be filled with the knowledge of the glory of the LORD, as the waters cover the sea (Hab. 2:14). There shall be no end to the government of God being established on the earth. My passion is that the part of the earth where he has placed me—the nation where He raised me up, can be restored completely to Him as people are redeemed in every sphere of life.

God gave me the privilege to have a church and to pastor His people, to direct them, help them know their purpose and maximize each of the potentials of the Kingdom that are in them to reclaim the earth. I am diligently teaching them that their priority in life is redeeming the land back to God who is its rightful Owner. So it is not a big deal that I am pastoring 25,000 people. How can I count that success when there are 4 million

257

souls in my city that are not all saved? That is a harvest field I cannot reap alone.

The passion of God is to restore and reclaim the whole earth. He died for that. So, I must maximize the potential of every member, to help him or her realize that they have the Kingdom within them and that they are the agents of that Kingdom. Their purpose is to become spiritual leaven to permeate the whole world, to be salt to preserve the truth and righteousness of the Kingdom, and to shine as light in the darkness of every human sphere of life.

When we pray "Thy kingdom come. Thy will be done" it means that we are willing to become the answer to God's heart cry. We surrender to allow His divine love to flow through us to conquer every enemy that resists His Kingdom reality. And Christ's Great Commission becomes ours.

According to the Joshua Project statistics, there are 16,304 people groups recognized globally. Of those, 6,652 are considered to still be unreached people groups, or 40.8% of all people of the world. With the current world population of 7.3 billion, that means there are 2.72 billion people in the world today who have not heard the gospel message. How small is our personal world? Are we seeking our own pleasure? Or are we willing to be an instrument of redemption, restoring the Kingdom of God to the earth?

THE REIGN OF LOVE

Can you imagine everyone in your church identifying his or her own territory to redeem it for the Kingdom —making it look like and function according to the principles of the Kingdom of God? What would happen in your community if every member of your church dedicates his or her self to extending the reign of God's love, His integrity and righteousness in their sphere of influence? No one can fulfill this calling alone. That is why the body of Christ on the earth —the church— is such a wonderful reality. With Christ as the Head, dwelling within each believer and empowering us, we can realize the "hope of glory". That hope is fulfilled when the Kingdom of God extends to all the earth.

I identified the love of God as a foundational principle of the Kingdom earlier in this book (See chapter 4). Because love is the nature and essence of who God is, we can also refer to love as the climate of the Kingdom. Love must become the air we breathe and the essence of our being. The scripture is clear that we have a capacity for love because of God's love for us:

> Now hope does not disappoint, because the love of God has been poured out in our hearts by the Holy Spirit who was given to us. For when we were still without strength, in due time Christ died for the ungodly. For scarcely for a righteous man will one die; yet perhaps for a good man someone would even dare to die. But God demonstrates His own love toward us, in that while we were still sinners, Christ died for us.
>
> **—ROMANS 5:5–8**

Our love is in response to the love Christ displayed for us, when we were still sinners. The apostle John states this fact bluntly: "We love Him because He first loved us" (1 John 4:19). When Jesus gave us a new commandment to love one another, He knew that it was His love for us that gave us a capacity to love others. And He was teaching the truth of the two dimensions of love: love for God and love for your neighbor. When one of the scribes asked Jesus which is the first commandment of all, Jesus answered him:

> The first of all the commandments is: Hear, O Israel, the LORD our God, the LORD is one. And you shall love the LORD your God with all your heart, with all your soul, with all your mind, and with all your strength. This is the first commandment. And the second, like it, is this: You shall love your neighbor as yourself. There is no other commandment greater than these.
>
> **—MARK 12:29–31**

Jesus knew that all the commandments of the Law of Moses rested on these two—loving God and loving your neighbor. They are the two dimensions of love that cannot exist without the other. For example, if you are filled with the love of God, you will not murder, steal, or lie. And if you love your brother, you will not covet what is his.

When you realize that God loves you as the undeserving sinner you are and you experience the peace and joy His loves brings to your heart, you cannot help loving others. In fact, the apostle John wrote that you do not love God if you do not love your brother:

> If someone says, 'I love God,' and hates his brother, he is a liar; for he who does not love his brother whom he has seen, how can he love God whom he has not seen? And this commandment we have from Him: that he who loves God must love his brother also.
>
> **—1 JOHN 4:20–21**

Loving God is an act; it is a display of the heart, a play scenario written in the spirit of man. Love can only be generated from the depths of the human heart. The apostle Paul explained this when he wrote, "For the love of Christ compels us, because we judge thus: that if One died for all, then all died; and He died for all, that those who live should live no longer for themselves, but for Him who died for them and rose again" (2 Cor. 5: 14–16. We can't pretend to love; love is a compelling force that will manifest itself in loving attitudes and acts.

Loving God is an act, it is a display of the heart.

When I receive the love of God and allow it to be poured into my life, I can say with Paul: "I have been crucified with Christ; it is no longer I who live, but Christ lives in me; and the life which I now live in the flesh I live by faith in the Son of God, who loved me and gave Himself for me" (Gal. 2:20).

When the love of God becomes our life, the scriptures declare that nothing can separate us from that love—not tribulation, distress, persecution, famine, nakedness or peril or sword (Rom. 5:35). I lose my ego-centric motivation when I choose to allow Christ to live in me. I don't need to live anymore, because I don't have life except for His which He gave for me for a ransom. God is not looking at my abilities, talents, or self-worth to qualify me to be His disciple. He only looks at my heart to see if I am surrendering to His love.

When the love of God reigns in our hearts, our lives will reflect His glory and power. Just as God expressed His great love by giving His Son to die for our redemption, so we will express our love for God by giving to others. When we love people, we will serve them as Christ did. He taught us: "Greater love has no one than this, than to lay down one's life for his friends" (Jn 1513). Loving God and loving people sets us free from the "It's all about me" syndrome. And we find true fulfillment and satisfaction when we are motivated by God's love to extend His Kingdom on the earth.

Discovering your personal promised land may not be an easy task. It will require seeking God earnestly until your heart is consumed with a passion to know Him. But the journey into God's heart will lead you into such depths of love as you have never dreamed possible. Then, all of life becomes an expression of that love, not a duty to fulfill. Motivated by divine love, there is nothing that is impossible for you. You begin to see the world in brilliant Technicolor; your personal promised land becomes your platform to share the love of God with others.

I pray for you, dear reader that you will discover the absolute wonder of God's love for you and His calling and destiny that He has prepared for you. If that is your desire, I encourage you to pray with me:

KINGDOM PRAYER

Dear Jesus, Thank you for displaying your great love for me at Calvary. I don't want to live any longer with my egocentric motivation. I want to be filled with your love, to love you and to love my neighbor. Let my heart be filled with that passionate love that compelled you to give your life for me. Help me to discover my promised land and to be empowered to extend your Kingdom into that place of influence. Show me what I need to leave behind to move forward in your will for my life. I choose to seek you until I hear your heartbeat and am filled with your love and passion for the harvest. I want to display your love to lost souls and reflect your glory throughout the earth. In your name I pray, amen.

KINGDOM PRINCIPLES
FROM CHAPTER 8

1. Every generation must reclaim their generation for God.
2. In this current generation, the church is not prospering in its mandate to extend Kingdom principles throughout culture.
3. For a large majority of youth raised in church, the church has become irrelevant to their goals and pursuits in life.
4. The amazing criteria by which Christ will judge nations is whether or not they fed the hungry, gave water to the thirsty, showed hospitality to strangers, clothed the naked, and visited the sick and those in prison.
5. To be successful according to the criteria Christ uses to judge nations, the church must leave the four walls behind which it cloisters its saints.
6. When God created the earth, He intended that everything that has breath would praise Him and enjoy relationship with the Creator.
7. The church must integrate into the environment and be involved in all the seven spheres of life, extending the virtues and principles and lifestyle of the Kingdom of God.
8. Your destiny will be fulfilled as you extend Kingdom

principles and lifestyle on the earth.

9. Jesus knew that all the commandments of the Law of Moses rested on these two—loving God and loving your neighbor. They are the two dimensions of love that cannot exist without the other.

10. Just as God expressed His great love by giving His Son to die for our redemption, so we will express our love for God by giving to others.

Chapter 9

THE PRESENTATION OF THE NATIONS BACK TO THE KINGDOM

Then the seventh angel sounded: And there were loud voices in heaven, saying, 'The kingdoms of this world have become the kingdoms of our Lord and of His Christ, and He shall reign forever and ever!'

—REVELATION 11:15

It is my prayer, as you have finished reading the previous chapters and praying the prayers included there with me, that God has done a work in your heart. My burden is that believers everywhere will be challenged to discover their promised land and find the fulfillment and fruitfulness God ordained for you. And for those who are working in their harvest field, I pray that your eyes will be opened to greater possibilities than you have imagined possible.

To that end, I want to share a little of my journey with you, to encourage you that no one is a more unlikely candidate than I for reaping a harvest among the nations. The heartbeat of God burns with longing for the redemption of every individual. He longs to see families and communities restored to the Kingdom of God, to experience the depths of his love and to be filled with the glory of God. But His great heart of love cannot be satisfied until He sees the nations that He loves bowing in worship before Him. Listen to the cry of His heart in these prophetic words of scripture:

> All the ends of the world shall remember and turn to the LORD, and all the families of the nations shall worship before You. For the kingdom is the LORD's, and He rules over the nations.
>
> **—PSALM 22:27–28**

> God be merciful to us and bless us, and cause His face to shine upon us, that Your way may be known on earth, Your salvation among all nations…Oh, let the nations be glad and sing for joy! For You shall judge the people righteously, and govern the nations on earth.
>
> **—PSALM 67:1–2, 4**

So many Christians are struggling in their personal walk with God, while others are trying to resolve family problems. Pastors are over-extended taking care of a few hundred "sheep" in their church. Yet, God is concerned with the salvation of nations. Why are we so unconcerned with the great desire of God's heart? Why is the church failing so miserably in impacting the nations of the earth?

It is not God's power that is lacking to accomplish the redemption of nations. And it is not His great love that falls short of the goal. Sadly, it is a lack of vision and passion on the part of His redeemed children that keeps the nations bound in darkness of false religions, lust for power, greed, and every form of human degradation known today.

While my journey is far from complete, it has removed me from a focus on my own personal struggles into ever increasing vision and passion for the redemption of the nations. With every new encounter with God, as I live a life of prayer and fasting, I feel the ache in His loving heart more deeply for the redemption of the earth. And with this increase in vision and passion has come the wisdom and empowerment to reap the harvest in many nations. Not alone, of course. We are not called to bring redemption to the nations single handedly. But God shows us His plan, connects us with others who inspire us and connects us to those whom we can inspire to greatness. Together we extend the Kingdom of God. Together we witness the miracle of redemption spreading like leaven throughout regions of the earth.

THE BEGINNING

As a Nigerian youth, shortly after I surrendered my life to God, I was notified that I had received a state scholarship and that I could choose to leave Nigeria to study in the U.S.A. or the USSR. When I consulted with my pastor, he told me to pray for direction. Later, we continued our conversation, and he gave me this word of wisdom, "If you survive in the Soviet Union, you will survive anywhere". I received his counsel and decided to go to the Soviet Union to study journalism at the Belarussian University.

Of course, I did not speak Russian. It was very difficult for me to learn the Russian language, which I had to do in order to study for my degree in journalism in a Russian University. My prospects for success seemed bleak even to my Russian professor. He told me, after several months of slow progress, that he knew I was a believer. He said that he was an atheist. And he told me that if I ever learned to speak Russian, he would light a candle in a Russian Orthodox Church. So great was his confidence in my ability to fail in that pursuit.

Rather than discourage me, those words became a challenge to me. I remembered my sister's words to me that whenever life seemed difficult, I should remember the promise of Deuteronomy 28:13: "And the LORD will make you the head and not the tail; you shall be above only, and not be beneath, if you heed the commandments of the LORD your God, which I command you today, and are careful to observe them."

I redoubled my efforts to study Russian, spending long hours in the library after completing my other classes. By the time I graduated, I had become one of the best students in my Faculty Preparation Group. Though my Russian professor did not light a candle as he had said he would, he unwittingly gave me the inspiration I needed to conquer that great obstacle to my destiny—mastering the Russian language.

UNLIKELY PROSPECT

Still, I did not understand why God had sent me to that cold, grey country. How can people be so ungodly? I wondered. Black people were not welcome there. I have been called ugly names and scorned in public because of my race. And it was understood that people could be sentenced to jail for their faith in God. I was attending an underground church where we gathered secretly to pray.

When I expressed my regrets to my Christian friends, they

encouraged me to seek God for His plan for my life, saying that God had brought me there for a reason. As I sought God, I cried out, "Why did You bring me to this country, Lord? Please answer me! For many days that was my only prayer.

Then something incredible happened. I had an amazing dream, which I dreamed three nights in a row. In the dream, I saw Jesus Himself coming to me and He took me by the hand to led me into my future. I saw myself standing on a stage near a preacher who was very well known at the time, and behind us were a group of key Christian leaders. Jesus came to me, took the microphone out of that preacher's hands, gave it to me and I began to preach to the great multitude of people there, mostly Europeans. Jesus stood beside me and began to show me sicknesses and problems the people were suffering. As I addressed each person, they immediately received an answer to their problem. I saw a paralyzed woman stand up from her wheelchair. And I saw a blind man receive his sight. There was no end to the miracles and healings I saw in the dream.

I saw Jesus Himself coming to me.

On the third night, when the dream was especially vivid, I awoke startled and heard a soft voice tell me to open my Bible. As I randomly opened the Word, I read from Isaiah, "The Spirit of the Lord God is upon me, because the Lord has anointed and qualified me to preach the gospel of good tidings to the meek, the poor, and afflicted; He has sent me to bind up and heal the brokenhearted, to proclaim liberty to the [physical and spiritual] captives and the opening of the prison and of the eyes to those who are bound" (Isa. 61:1AMP). The words engulfed me like a mighty wave; every cell of my body was singing in a thousand voices that seemed to be filling the room. I wondered if my roommates heard anything.

I began to panic at the prospect of being involved in what the dream seemed to indicate. I was only 19 years old and had just been a believer for a few months. With these thoughts filling my mind, I felt impressed to read Jeremiah chapter 1, where the Lord answered those questioning doubts:

> But the LORD said to me: Do not say, 'I am a youth,' For you shall go to all to whom I send you, and whatever I command you, you shall speak. Do not be afraid of their faces, for I am with you to deliver you, says the Lord.
>
> **—JEREMIAH 1:8**

PERSECUTION BEGINS

Not long after that experience, I heard loud banging on my dormitory door. When I answered it, I saw the dean of the preparatory department along with the Communists party secretary for the dormitory. They were there to take down the picture of Jesus that I had hung above my bed. I was given the choice to be expelled and sent back to Africa or get rid of the picture. I was also reminded that I was in a communist country where the only religion was atheism. It was all right to be a believer in my heart, but the criminal code prohibited religious propaganda.

Once again, as when my atheistic Russian professor offered to burn a candle, I was challenged by this religious persecution. I promised myself that I would serve God in such a way that people would know that Christ had given His life for them to set them free from the national darkness of atheism. God was finding a way to put His compassion in my heart for the Soviet people, and I determined to tell them His wonderful truth about a life in the Kingdom of Love, Joy, and Peace.

God was finding a way to put His compassion in my heart for the Soviet people.

I spent 7 years in Belarus, where I mastered the Russian language and completed a Master's Degree in Journalism, with honors. During my final years there, when the political climate relaxed a little, my Christian friends and I began to go on evangelistic trips to different cities and villages. As we traveled on our way to a town to minister, we would pray, sing, and prophesy during the entire trip, which could last for several hours.

When we arrived in a town or village, we didn't have to invite people to a meeting, because as soon as they saw black people, they came running. Many had never seen a black person, and at times, discrimination against us was intense. But we prayed for people and they were healed and received Christ as their Savior.

During this time, I established a church in Minsk that grew very fast, along with two other churches in the area that I helped to plant. We rented a hall across from a cancer hospital where people who got leukemia after the Chernobyl nuclear disaster came for treatment. We began to invite these cancer patients to our services. The patients would come to our meetings in their hospital attire, and some of them were healed of cancer. When the news spread, a TV crew from a popular youth organization visited one of our services. They interviewed me and broadcast a five-minute segment about our "Christian Youth Movement" as they called it. The program aired on Belarussian National Television. It was unheard of at the time to give free airtime to Christian activities and to present them in a positive light.

Then, in 1992 my passport was confiscated because of my

involvement in evangelism and I was advised to leave the country within two weeks. During that time, I received a message that a commercial TV channel in Kyiv (partially owned by a Christian missionary) was looking for a representative in Ukraine. The qualifications for the position were to be a believer, to know Russian and English, and to have a degree in journalism. God had prepared me uniquely for those prerequisites.

God had prepared me uniquely for those prerequisites.

A NEW BEGINNING

I was accepted for the position in Kyiv, and started working at the TV station, producing Christian programs and preaching television sermons viewed by many residents of Kyiv for almost a whole year. Though I was enjoying my life as a journalist, God began to call me to plant a church in Kyiv. It had been very painful to me to have to give up my churches in Belarus, and I did not want to start another church for that reason.

Reluctantly, I began to seek God in prayer and fasting for four to six hours a day from July to September. Out of that encounter with God, I understood that I was to begin a home Bible study. I announced on TV that I was starting a Bible group in my home. I began with 7 people. Five of those seven people eventually became faithful, effective ministers of God.

On February 6, 1994, my evangelistic team held our first three-day crusade in Kyiv, which resulted in the establishing of the Word of Faith Church. It would later become the Embassy of God. We began with 49 people. I established a goal to win 100 people a month to the Lord in that city. The spiritual darkness was incredible during those first years. I saw it as a huge dark cloud over the entire city. I cried out to the Lord to raise up a person to remove that cloud. Through much prayer and fasting, we have seen that dark cloud disappear; we have become an instrumental part of the answer to that cry.

THE INCREDIBLE HAPPENS

After I moved to Kyiv, I was still praying that God would give me the wife that He had planned for me. You can read the story of our romance in my book, Olorunwa, The Roads of Life. God did bring me a beautiful, godly wife, and has given us three beautiful children. Though the ministry has required that I travel extensively, I have made my family a priority and have determined to make time for them. My wife, Bose, and I cooperate in all family matters. We are happily married and have been able to help others through our testimony, published in a book called Successful Marriage Takes Work (Fares Publishing House, 2007, Kiev).

What has happened in the last 20 years, which I have referred to briefly in this text, can only be described as a miracle. Besides our mega church in Ukraine, which currently has 25,000 members, there have been over 1000 churches planted in 50 nations during these years. In an interview by the "Washington Post", they described me as:

> ...a black man in the country noted for its rampant racism, a protestant in a country known as the birthplace of the Russian Orthodox Church. He is a foreigner whose vibrant style of preaching accompanied with electronic keyboards and pretty girls dancing and singing on the stage somehow clashes with the traditional and reserved view of faith that

Ukrainians adhere to…sharing the message of hope and redemption. [Olorunwa ("There is a God"): The Roads of Life, A Portrait of Sunday Adelaja, (Kyiv, Ukraine: Fares, 2007) p.110–111]

Persecution has continued as the influence of the church has increased in the city and in the nation. I am under close watch by the State Security Service, have been threatened by the mafia, have been the victim of several lawsuits. The newspaper has published articles accusing me of all kinds of sins, from having links to a financial ponsi scheme to drug dealing.

These are hardships that I willingly endure because I believe I am fulfilling the plan of God for my life. If I had chosen my desire, I would have served God in a protestant country where people honor preachers instead of insulting them and accusing them publicly of sins they have not committed. I have ministered in over 60 countries of the world and people don't treat me disrespectfully like they do in Ukraine.

But I came to Ukraine in obedience to God and these slanderous accusations are a humbling experience for me. They are part of the sacrifice I give to God, denying myself and taking up my cross to follow Him. And I view my accusers, not as my enemies, but as catalysts that propel me forward to fulfill the passion of God's heart and defeat His enemies. I bless these "enemies" with the love of God and I pray for the people of Ukraine that God will forgive them, show mercy to them, and save them.

I view my accusers as catalysts that propel me forward.

Today, despite all the slander and false accusations against me in Ukraine and all over the world, the Kingdom of God keeps on advancing with force.

"And from the days of John the Baptist until now the Kingdom of heaven suffers violence, and the violent take it by force."

MATTHEW 11:12

The following statistics of the Embassy of God Church reflect the reality that God is building His church and the gates of hell will not prevail against it. In 15 years, beginning from nothing, the following has been achieved by the grace of God:

Embassy of God Church has raised up:

- 2000 churches in 50 countries
- 35 Churches in Kiev, more than 25,000 memebers
- Over 200 rehabilitaion centers for drug and alcohol addicts
- 5,000 people have been set free from addiction
- 600 NGOs
- 260 schools from which more than 23,000 people have graduated
- Trust Line, where thousands of phone calls are received from people asking for help

I want to encourage you that any church, any community of believers that are joined for the common purpose of extending the Kingdom, can achieve these kinds of influence and statistics. When the church leaves the four walls, miracles happen, the city is impacted and the Kingdom reigns with power. I challenge you to dare to "do church" in a new way.

TEACHING KINGDOM PRINCIPLES

As a pastor of a local church, my heart is burdened for the end-time harvest that I believe is to become a worldwide revival. While I am encouraged at the wonderful results we are having in our church in Kiev, Ukraine, I long to see those same results and greater revival come to my precious brothers and sisters in other nations as well.

As I mentioned, in my church in Kiev over 2,000,000 people have given their hearts to Christ at our altar. This harvest of souls has not come through large crusades or other conventional evangelism "methods." It is a direct result of teaching my congregation these principles of the Kingdom. They understand that their priority in life is to develop a lifestyle that will "leaven" the sphere of society where they are called to minister—to reap a harvest and restore the Kingdom of God to the earth.

All new converts who come to the church receive instruction through training classes that help them discover their personal mandate as a Christian to extend the principles and lifestyle of the Kingdom on the earth. They understand that their purpose as a believer is to restore the glory of God to the earth. They are taught practically how to live a Christian life and are instructed in the God-given purpose for which they were born. We help them to discover their "promised land" and motivate them to extend the Kingdom of God in that sphere of influence.

New converts are not encouraged simply to become choir members or ushers, or to pursue classical ministry as a pastor. Of course, if they have these giftings and desire to serve, they should do so. Service in local churches is a natural function for every believer, which is important for their growth in God. And if God calls some to become pastors, we equip them to that end. But the goal of our local church for new believers is not to fill their time in organized church activities and programs.

It is the responsibility of the local church to teach believers Kingdom principles to equip them to do the work of the ministry in their sphere of influence. We teach them that every person is born to fulfill a particular purpose in extending the Kingdom of God on the earth. Their purpose in life is to develop a lifestyle that will make them salt and light on the earth. Their passion must be to become the person Christ intended for them to be to carry His Kingdom into a godless society and reclaim it, filling the earth with His glory.

That is why Jesus said to seek first the Kingdom. When you are born-again, you are brought into the Kingdom to find your destiny to help increase the Kingdom on the earth. In my church, I train new believers that they are here for only one purpose, which is to advance the Kingdom. I teach them that salvation does not just assure you of having your sins forgiven and your peace with God restored. It presents you as well with the responsibility to deny yourself, to take your "ego" off the throne of your life and to acknowledge the lordship of Jesus. Without apology, Jesus declared, "If anyone desires to come after Me, let him deny himself, and take up his cross, and follow Me." (Matt. 16:24).

The apostle Paul echoed this reality when he declared, "I die daily" (1 Cor. 15:31). And he explained his selfless motivation for living out these words: "I have been crucified with Christ; it is no longer I who live, but Christ lives in me; and the life which I now live in the flesh I live by faith in the Son of God, who loved me and gave Himself for me (Gal. 2:20). Paul understood that he could no longer live for himself, his own purposes or pleasure. His life was surrendered to the Christ within, who would be glorified and His government increased through Paul's actions.

FOCUSED ON THE KINGDOM

The purpose of every Christian is the same: to glorify Christ and extend His Kingdom on the earth, to bring it into alignment with His will. But because the world is so vast, he has given certain talents, abilities, and gifts to each individual, which makes them unique. No two people are alike and each person has a specific calling, a designated assignment or mission to take dominion of his or her promised land and advance the government of God on the earth.

Everyone has a passion for something. When I have conversations with my members, I ask them what their passion is; what part of the world they are redeeming back for God. What is their promised land into which they focus on bringing the Kingdom lifestyle? Because we train believers to seek first the Kingdom and to discover their personal destiny, it is unusual that one of them would not know his or her mission in life. They are on a journey to discover where they are to be involved to restore the Kingdom of God to the earth.

A majority of my members will be able to respond specifically to those questions, unless they are brand new believers. In that case, they are encouraged to enroll in the "School of Discovery" we have established to teach them how to discover their mission as a Christian to be a God-carrier. They understand that salvation does not just involve receiving Christ to be forgiven of their sins so they can go to heaven. He placed the Kingdom inside of them because He has a mission for them to accomplish. As believers, we are His resources and He does not waste His resources.

TEAMWORK FOR SUCCESS!

You don't do your vision alone. Reaping the harvest is not about one person with a vision struggling to make a mark in any sphere of influence; it is about multiplication of vision and laborers who can carry out that vision in a much shorter time and more effectively. To reclaim a region for the Kingdom, it is necessary to work together with others who have the same burden.

For example, the lady in our church who is reaching into the sphere of education and speaking to students using her morality curriculum is training a team to work with her. She will never be able to reclaim the whole sphere of education in our city alone. So we train others who have the personal burden for redeeming the educational system by establishing the principles of the Kingdom in the lives of students and teachers.

They have a list of 350 schools in our area and their agenda is to be able to get into every school with their programs to gradually bring the influence of the Kingdom of God to each one. We are not trying to claim only one school; we are working to reclaim every school age child for the Kingdom of God. After that, we expect to do the same in every city in our nation. That is our strategy for reclaiming this generation for the Kingdom of God.

At first, she had a team of only ten people. And I told her there are too many schools to reach for such a small team; it will take too long. So we announced in church that anyone who has a burden for schools should attend her training classes. She presents a training school twice a year for a week to train people who are interested in going to schools for a week with her curriculum.

Every year she trains about 600 team members and gives them a recommendation and certificate that opens doors for them in the school system. Because she had already established a reputation in the schools for teaching children a curriculum of moral living and helping them think about strong, life choices, other schools are open to that curriculum. Now that the team is growing, we can be presenting these Kingdom principles in 100 schools at the same time.

When you establish outreaches like this in every sphere of life with more and more people functioning in their calling to reclaim their sphere for the Kingdom, many more people get saved. This living cycle continues with each new convert; they are empowered to discover their calling, get training, and are discipled to bring the Kingdom influence into their "world". In every sphere of life our church members are allowing God's love to shine through them and meeting the needs of people, bringing souls to Christ, one by one.

GREAT EXPECTATIONS

A Kingdom Driven Life is God's provision, His instrument on the earth to extend the Kingdom of heaven—the influence of the King—to all the earth. The church is the greatest platform for extending and promoting the Kingdom God throughout the earth. God established the church as the means to prepare believers to embrace the gospel of the Kingdom and become God-carriers, filled with faith and maturing in the character of Christ. His government must increase; the ultimate goal is that the church extend the principles of the Kingdom as the primary governing principles in the nations of the earth.

No one is created by God and called to His Kingdom simply to promote a ministry or build a strong church. Everyone is called to promote God and extend His dominion on the earth. Your goal as a pastor of a local church is to make your church a platform on which you preach the message of the Kingdom as the priority of life for every believer. According to the scriptures, you are to help every member of your church to discover their "promised land" and to become effective in permeating the earth like leaven, spreading the dominion of God's Kingdom everywhere.

Instead of cloistering themselves within the four walls of the church, believers need to wield their godly influence in every sphere of life where God calls them to serve. You might be called to excel in the high-tech world of computers. You may be called to be a businessman in the area of retail clothing. You may have found your calling in working the land to produce crops, or in education, sports, or in the world of media. You may reap a wonderful harvest in the social sphere where so many needy people are desperate to hear the good news of the gospel.

Don't ever doubt the power of God's greatness to impact that sphere with His Lordship, to infuse supernatural ideas and wisdom into your mind so that you will succeed and become the head and not the tail. He will give you authority in the area of your calling, so that no other power can hinder or eliminate you. The divine power that is in you cannot be stopped. As you get to know the source of that power, Christ in you the hope of glory, you will succeed above all others in your area of expertise. That power will make you reign in life through your sphere of influence, extending the principles of the Kingdom of God and conquering that territory for Him.

Don't limit the extent of your fruitfulness. You are given talents and gifts and the power of Almighty God is in you to be productive. You should never be satisfied with minimal productivity, but go forth and increase through multiplication, with the goal of transferring more citizens to the Kingdom and the goal that the principles of the Kingdom of God would be extended thoughout the entire earth.

In every sphere of life, as leaven that leavens the whole lump, you can become more than conquerors. You are trusted by God to go and take back the earth—the nations—for the King. To complete that assignment, He has made the unlimited power of

God available to you. You are the hope of the world. Those are not just words, their reality must be realized through your actions. That divine power is not to lie dormant within you through your ignorance or lack of understanding.

If the economy of your nation is to be revived and restored, it is your responsibility. If government is to enact laws that are based on godly standards, you will have to invade the political arena. You can't live in hope that unbelievers will restore the financial or political health of the country. You are anointed by God and entrusted with His power to do exploits. Go and compel the adoption of Kingdom principles in your business or other sphere of life. Go in faith to extend the domain of the King. Don't go to negotiate or compromise, or worse, to fail.

I have preached to my congregation that within ten years I expect the members of my church to be some of the most respected individuals in our country. Based on understanding the power of God working in us, that is not wishful thinking; it is reality. That should be our expectation because of the power of the Lord in us is to enable and to "give us all things that pertain to life and godliness" (2 Pet. 1:2)

The goal of the apostle Paul was not to establish churches or preach the gospel of Christ on the whole earth. His expectation was much loftier than that. He declared:

> ...Christ in you the hope of glory, whom we preach, warning every man, and teaching every man in all wisdom; that we may present every man perfect in Christ Jesus: Whereunto I also labour striving according to his working, which worketh in me mightily.
> **—COLOSSIANS 1:27—29**

That is why I will never be satisfied to have the largest church in Europe. I tell members of my church not to go out and boast that they are members of the biggest church in the country. Our goal is much greater than that. We are in His church planted in this nation to extend God's authority and bring this nation to the feet of the Lord Jesus. We labor to bring all to the knowledge of Christ so that we can equip every believer to become "perfect" in his destiny and calling on the earth. When every member of the church becomes effective in impacting their sphere of life to God, we will be true representatives of the body of Christ on the earth. Until we do that we have not even begun to fulfill our Kingdom purpose. Then, we will move forward to fulfill the great desire of God's heart for other nations as well. One day we will say with John the Revelator:

> After these things I looked, and behold, a great multitude which no one could number, of all nations, tribes, peoples, and tongues, standing before the throne and before the Lamb, clothed with white robes, with palm branches in their hands, and crying out with a loud voice, saying, 'Salvation belongs to our God who sits on the throne, and to the Lamb!'
>
> **—REVELATION 7:9–10**

If you are willing for your vision to be enlarged, to have greater expectations of the power of redemption working in your life, your family, your church, community, your nation, and the nations of the earth, I earnestly encourage you to pray this prayer with me:

KINGDOM PRAYER

Dear Lord Jesus, Please forgive me for not having greater expectations of the power of your grace working in and through me. Please let me know your heartbeat for the nations, for all the peoples of the earth. And let me be a part of reclaiming territory for Your Kingdom to come to earth. I surrender more completely to your sovereign will for my life, and determine to seek you until I am firmly planted in my "promised land". Help me to be an effective part of the Kingdom Driven Life, filled with revelation and knowledge of the passion of your loving heart. Let me be part of the answer to our Lord's petition, "Thy kingdom come, thy will be done in earth as it is in heaven." Thank you for answering this prayer. In your name I pray, amen.

KINGDOM PRINCIPLES
FROM CHAPTER 9

---

1. God's great heart of love cannot be satisfied until He sees the nations that He loves bowing in worship before Him

2. God was finding a way to put His compassion in my heart for the Soviet people, and I determined to tell them His wonderful truth about a life in the Kingdom of Love, Joy, and Peace.

3. As a pastor of a local church, my heart is burdened for the end-time harvest that I believe is to become a worldwide revival.

4. The harvest of souls in our church has not come through large crusades or other conventional evangelism "methods." It is a direct result of teaching my congregation the principles of the Kingdom.

5. We teach new converts that every person is born to fulfill a particular purpose in extending the Kingdom of God throughout the earth

6. When I have conversations with my members, I ask them what their passion is; what part of the world they are redeeming back for God.

7. A Kingdom Driven Life is God's provision, His instrument on the earth to extend the Kingdom of heaven—the

dominion of the King—to all the earth.

8. 8. Go and enforce the Kingdom principles in your business or other sphere of life. Go in faith to conquer. Don't go to negotiate or compromise, or worse, to fail.

9. We are in this church planted in this nation to extend God's Lordship and bring this nation to the feet of the Lord Jesus.

10. One day we will say with John the Revelator:

After these things I looked, and behold, a great multitude which no one could number, of all nations, tribes, peoples, and tongues, standing before the throne and before the Lamb, clothed with white robes, with palm branches in their hands, and crying out with a loud voice, saying, 'Salvation belongs to our God who sits on the throne, and to the Lamb!'

—REVELATION 7:9–10

Amen.

ABOUT PASTOR
SUNDAY ADELAJA

S unday Adelaja is the founder and senior pastor of the Embassy of God in Kiev Ukraine and the author of more than 300 books which are translated in several languages including Chinese, German, French, Arabic, etc.

A fatherless child from a 40 hut village in Nigeria, Sunday was recruited by communist Russia to ignite a revolution, instead he was saved just before leaving for the USSR where he secretly trained himself in the Bible while earning a Master's degree in journalism. By age thirty-three he had built the largest church in Europe.

Today, his church in Kiev has planted over a thousand daughter churches in over fifty countries of the world. Right now they plant four new churches every week. He is known to be the only person in the world pastoring a cross cultural church where 99% of his twenty five thousand members are white Caucasians.

His work has been widely reported by world media outlets like Washington Post, The wall street Journal, Forbes, New York times, Associated Press, Reuters, CNN, BBC, German, Dutch, French National television, etc.

Pastor Sunday had the opportunity to speak on a number of occasions in the United Nations. In 2007 he had the rare privilege of opening the United States Senate with prayers. He has spoken in the Israeli Knesset and the Japanese parliament along with several other countries. Pastor Sunday is known as an expert in national transformation through biblical principles and values.

Pastor Sunday is happily married to his "princess' Pastor Bose Adelaja. They are blessed with three children, Perez, Zoe and Pearl.

BOOKS BY PASTOR SUNDAY ADELAJA

Churchshift: *Revolutionlize you faith, Church and life for the 21st Century.*

Money Won't Make you Rich: *God's Principles for True Wealth, Prosperity and Success.*

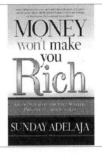

Time is Life: *History Makers Honor Time.*

Pastoring Without Tears: *It is possible to live and minister without sorrow and grief .*

Olorunwa (There is God): *Portrait of Sunday Adelaja. THE ROADS OF LIFE.*

Dearly beloved!

Warm greetings to you in the name of our Lord Jesus Christ!

I have been a pastor for over 20 years, and I have realized that majority of Christians around the world do not comprehend, that it is not enough to just pray and fast to bring God's Kingdom to the earth. Most Christians have this misconception, in the sense that they take into account only the spiritual aspects. They do not understand the importance of working intensively on themselves, and how to take the kingdom of God beyond the church's walls.

That is why I decided to give a chance to all my followers and mentees to become part of a renewed Mentorship Program with me.

I am sure, that participation in this Mentorship Program will give you an opportunity

- Make your goals more precise, concrete and real
- Build a system that would enable you reach your goals
- Arrange important and urgent tasks according to priorities
- Learn how to become influential in your sphere, in order to promote the Kingdom
- and its values
- Learn how to manage your time and your life
- Increase the effectiveness and efficiency of your work
- Learn how to live an effective Kingdom-based life
- Have monthly guidance and support from me as a Pastor, leader, mentor and father

For those of you, who had previously participated in this

program, I would like to tell you that my team and I have been working hard to improve on it. I want to strongly encourage you to continue your participation, and be prepared for a more intensive program.

When you sign up for the renewed Mentorship Program, you will get:

• Monthly letters with a topic that we will be working on for the next 30 days

• Video messages that I'd be recording for all my mentees

• Assignments for practical work on what we've learned

Therefore, if you are interested in joining this program, please fill out the form on this page: http://www.sundayadelajablog.com/mentorship

God bless.
Yours in Christ,
Pastor Sunday Adelaja.
www.sundayadelajablog.com

FOLLOW PASTOR SUNDAY ON SOCIAL MEDIA

Subscribe And Read Pastor Sunday's Blog:
WWW.SUNDAYADELAJABLOG.COM

Follow These Links And Listen To Over 200 Of Pastor Sunday`S Messages Free Of Charge:
WWW.GODEMBASSY.COM/MEDIA

Follow Pastor Sunday On Twitter, 5 Words Of Wisdom Daily:
WWW.TWITTER.COM/SUNDAYADELAJA
…And Suggest Your Friends To Follow As Well!

Join Pastor Sunday's Facebook Page To Stay In Touch:
WWW.FACEBOOK.COM/PASTOR.SUNDAY.ADELAJA
…And Suggest Your Friends To Join As Well!

VISIT OUR WEBSITES FOR MORE INFORMATION ABOUT PASTOR SUNDAY'S MINISTRY:
http://www.godembassy.com
http://www.pastorsunday.com
http://www.churchshift.org
http://sundayadelaja.de
http://sundayadelaja.com
http://www.adelaja.com

CONTACT

For distribution or to order bulk copies of this book, please contact us:

USA
CORNERSTONE PUBLISHING
info@thecornerstonepublishers.com
+1 (516) 547-4999 . www.thecornerstonepublishers.com

AFRICA
Sunday Adelaja Media Ltd.
Email: btawolana@hotmail.com
+2348187518530, +2348097721451, +2348034093699.

LONDON, UK
Pastor Abraham Great
abrahamagreat@gmail.com
+447711399828, +44-1908538141

KIEV, UKRAINE
pa@godembassy.org
Mobile: +380674401958

NOTE

NOTE